PLOTINUS

ENNEAD I.1

THE *ENNEADS* OF PLOTINUS

With Philosophical Commentaries

Series Editors: John M. Dillon, Trinity College, Dublin and Andrew Smith, University College, Dublin

Also Available in the Series:

I.6: *On Beauty* by Andrew Smith

II.5: *On What Is Potentially and What Actually* by Cinzia Arruzza

II.9: *Against the Gnostics* by Sebastian Ramon Philipp Gertz

IV.3–4.29: *Problems Concerning the Soul* by John M. Dillon & H. J. Blumenthal

IV.4.30–45 & IV.5: *Problems Concerning the Soul* by Gary Gurtler

IV.7: *On the Immortality of the Soul* by Barrie Fleet

IV.8: *On the Descent of the Soul Into Bodies* by Barrie Fleet

V.1: *On the Three Primary Levels of Reality* by Eric D. Perl

V.5: *That the Intelligibles are not External to Intellect, and on the Good* by Lloyd P. Gerson

VI.4 & VI.5: *On the Presence of Being, One and the Same, Everywhere as a Whole* by Eyjólfur Emilsson & Steven Strange

VI.8: *On the Voluntary and on the Free Will of the One* by Kevin Corrigan and John D. Turner

Forthcoming Titles in the Series include:

I.2: *On Virtues* by Suzanne Stern-Gillet

I.3: *On Dialectic* by Pauliina Remes

I.4: *On Well-Being* by Kieran McGroarty

I.5: *On Whether Well Being Increases With Time* by Danielle A. Layne

I.8: *On the Nature and Source of Evil* by Anne Sheppard

II.4: *On Matter* by Anthony A. Long

II.7: *On Complete Blending* by Robert Goulding

II.8: *On Sight* by Robert Goulding

III.4: *On Our Allotted Guardian Spirit* by Wiebke-Marie Stock

III.5: *On Love* by Sara Magrin

III.6: *On Impassibility* by Eleni Perdikouri

III.7: *On Eternity and Time* by László Bene

III.8: *On Nature and Contemplation* by George Karamanolis

IV.6: *On Sense-Perception and Memory* by Peter Lautner

V.2, **V.4**, and **V.6**: *On the One and Intellect* by Eleni Perdikouri

V.3: *On the Knowing Hypostases* by Marie-Élise Zovko

V.8: *On Intelligible Beauty* by Andrew Smith

V.9: *On Intellect, Ideas, and Being* by Matthias Vorwerk

VI.1–2: *On the Genera of Being (I+II)* by Damien Caluori & Regina Füchslin

VI.3: *On the Genera of Being (III)* by Riccardo Chiaradonna

VI.7: *The Forms and the Good* by Nicholas Banner

VI.9: *On the Good or the One* by Stephen R. L. Clark

PLOTINUS
ENNEAD I.1

What is the Living Thing?
What is Man?

Translation with an Introduction
and Commentary

GERARD O'DALY

PARMENIDES
PUBLISHING

Las Vegas | Zurich | Athens

PARMENIDES PUBLISHING
Las Vegas | Zurich | Athens

This edition published in 2017 by Parmenides Publishing
in the United States of America

ISBN soft cover: 978-1-930972-98-8
ISBN e-Book: 978-1-930972-99-5

Library of Congress Cataloging-in-Publication Data

Names: Plotinus, author. | O'Daly, Gerard J. P.
Title: Ennead I.1 : what is the living thing? what is man? / Plotinus ; translation with an introduction and commentary Gerard O'Daly.
Other titles: Ennead. I,1. English | What is the living thing? What is man?
Description: Las Vegas : Parmenides Publishing, 2017. | Series: The Enneads of Plotinus with philosophical commentaries | Includes bibliographical references and indexes. |
Identifiers: LCCN 2017028632 (print) | LCCN 2017044137 (ebook) | ISBN 9781930972995 (ebook) | ISBN 9781930972988 (pbk. : alk. paper) | ISBN 9781930972995 (e-book)
Subjects: LCSH: Plotinus. Ennead. I, 1. | Soul--Early works to 1800. | Ethics, Ancient--Early works to 1800.
Classification: LCC B693.E52 (ebook) | LCC B693.E52 E5 2017c (print) | DDC »186/.4--dc23
LC record available at https://lccn.loc.gov/2017028632

Typeset in Warnock and Futura by Parmenides Publishing
Printed by Edwards Brothers Malloy, Chicago, IL
www.edwardsbrothersmalloy.com

www.parmenides.com

To
Albrecht Dihle
mentor and friend

Contents

Introduction to the Series 1
Abbreviations 11
Preface and Acknowledgments 15
INTRODUCTION TO THE TREATISE 17
Note on the Greek Text 31
Synopsis 33
TRANSLATION 47
COMMENTARY 65
Chapter 1 66
Chapter 2 72
Chapter 3 84
Chapter 4 97
Chapter 5 104
Chapter 6 112
Chapter 7 116
Chapter 8 126
Chapter 9 135

Chapter 10 144
Chapter 11 152
Chapter 12 166
Chapter 13 180
Select Bibliography 185
Index of Ancient Authors 201
Index of Names and Subjects 207

Introduction to the Series With a Brief Outline of the Life and Thought of Plotinus (205–270 CE)

PLOTINUS WAS BORN IN 205 CE in Egypt of Greek-speaking parents. He attended the philosophical schools in Alexandria where he would have studied Plato (427–347 BCE), Aristotle (384–322 BCE), the Stoics and Epicureans as well as other Greek philosophical traditions. He began his serious philosophical education, however, relatively late in life, at the age of twenty-seven and was deeply impressed by the Platonist Ammonius Saccas about whom we, unfortunately, know very little, but with whom Plotinus studied for some eleven years. Even our knowledge of Plotinus' life is limited to what we can glean from Porphyry's introduction to his edition of his philosophical treatises, an account colored by Porphyry's own concerns. After completing his studies in Alexandria Plotinus attempted, by joining a military expedition of the Roman emperor Gordian III, to make contact with the

Brahmins in order to learn something of Indian thought. Unfortunately Gordian was defeated and killed (244). Plotinus somehow managed to extract himself and we next hear of him in Rome where he was able to set up a school of philosophy in the house of a high-ranking Roman lady by the name of Gemina. It is, perhaps, surprising that he had no formal contacts with the Platonic Academy in Athens, which was headed at the time by Longinus, but Longinus was familiar with his work, partly at least through Porphyry who had studied in Athens. The fact that it was Rome where Plotinus set up his school may be due to the originality of his philosophical activity and to his patrons. He clearly had some influential contacts, not least with the philhellenic emperor Gallienus (253–268), who may also have encouraged his later failed attempt to set up a civic community based on Platonic principles in a ruined city in Campania.

Plotinus' school was, like most ancient schools of philosophy, relatively small in scale, but did attract distinguished students from abroad and from the Roman upper classes. It included not only philosophers but also politicians and members of the medical profession who wished to lead the philosophical life. His most famous student was Porphyry (233–305) who, as a relative latecomer to the school, persuaded him to put into writing the results of his seminars. It is almost certain that we possess most, if not all, of his written output, which represents his mature thought, since he didn't commence writing until the age of forty-eight. The school seemingly had inner and outer circles, and Plotinus himself was clearly an inspiring and sympathetic teacher who took a deep interest in the philosophical and spiritual progress of his students. Porphyry tells us that when he was suffering from severe depression Plotinus straight away visited him in his lodgings to help him. His concern for others is also illustrated by the fact that he was entrusted with the personal education of many orphans and the care of their property and careers. The reconciliation of this worldly involvement with the encouragement to lead a life of contemplation is encapsulated in Porphyry's comment that "he was present to himself and others at the same time."

The *Enneads* of Plotinus is the edition of his treatises arranged by his pupil Porphyry who tried to put shape to the collection he had inherited by organizing it into six sets of nine treatises (hence the name *"Enneads")* that led the reader through the levels of Plotinus' universe, from the physical world to Soul, Intellect and, finally, to the highest principle, the One. Although Plotinus undoubtedly had a clearly structured metaphysical system by the time he began committing himself to expressing his thought in written form, the treatises themselves are not systematic expositions, but rather explorations of particular themes and issues raised in interpreting Plato and other philosophical texts read in the School. In fact, to achieve his neat arrangement Porphyry was sometimes driven even to dividing certain treatises (e.g., III.2–3; IV.3–5, and VI.4–5).

Although Plotinus' writings are not transcripts of his seminars, but are directed to the reader, they do, nevertheless, convey the sort of lively debate that he encouraged in his school. Frequently he takes for granted that a particular set of ideas is already familiar as having been treated in an earlier seminar that may or may not be found in the written text. For this reason it is useful for the reader to have some idea of the main philosophical principles of his system as they can be extracted from the *Enneads* as a whole.

Plotinus regarded himself as a faithful interpreter of Plato whose thought lies at the core of his entire project. But Plato's thought, whilst definitive, does according to Plotinus require careful exposition and clarification, often in the light of other thinkers such as Aristotle and the Stoics. It is because of this creative application of different traditions of ancient thought to the interpretation of Plato that Plotinus' version of Platonism became, partly through the medium of later Platonists such as Porphyry, Iamblichus (245–325), and Proclus (412–485), an influential source and way of reading both Plato and Aristotle in the Middle Ages, the Renaissance, and up to the early 19th century, when scholars first began to differentiate Plato and "Neoplatonism." His thought, too, provided early Christian theologians of the Latin and particularly of the Byzantine tradition, with a rich variety of metaphysical concepts with which to explore and express difficult doctrinal ideas. His fashioning of Plato's ideas into a consistent metaphysical structure, though no longer accepted as a uniquely valid way of approaching Plato, was influential in promoting the notion of metaphysical systems in early modern philosophy. More recently increasing interest has centered on his exploration of the self, levels of consciousness, and his expansion of discourse beyond the levels of normal ontology to the examination of what lies both above and beneath being. His thought continues to challenge us when confronted with the issue of man's nature and role in the universe and of the extent and limitations of human knowledge.

Whilst much of Plotinus' metaphysical structure is recognizably an interpretation of Plato it is an interpretation that is not always immediately obvious just because it is filtered through several centuries of developing Platonic thought, itself already overlaid with important concepts drawn from other schools. It is, nevertheless, useful as a starting point to see how Plotinus attempts to bring coherence to what he believed to be a comprehensive worldview expressed in the Platonic dialogues. The Platonic Forms are central. They become for him an intelligible universe that is the source and model of the physical universe. But aware of Aristotle's criticism of the Platonic Forms as lifeless causes he takes on board Aristotle's concept of god as a self-thinker to enable him to identify this intelligible universe as a divine Intellect that thinks itself as the Forms or Intelligibles. The doctrine of the Forms as the thoughts of god had already entered Platonism, but not as the rigorously argued identity that Plotinus proposed. Moreover the Intelligibles, since they are identical with Intellect, are themselves actively intellectual; they are intellects. Thus Plato's world of Forms has become a complex and dynamic intelligible universe in which unity and plurality, stability, and activity are reconciled.

Now although the divine Intellect is one it also embraces plurality, both because its thoughts, the Intelligibles, are many and because it may itself be analyzed into thinker and thought. Its unity demands a further principle, which is the cause of its unity. This principle, which is the cause of all unity and being but does not possess unity or being in itself, he calls the One, an interpretation of the Idea of the Good in Plato's *Republic* that is "beyond being" and that may be seen as the simple (hence "one") source of all reality. We thus have the first two of what subsequently became known as the three Hypostases, the One, Intellect, and Soul, the last of which acts as an intermediary between the intelligible and physical universes. This last Hypostasis takes on all the functions of transmitting form and life that may be found in Plato, although Plato himself does not always make such a clear distinction between soul and intellect. Thus the One is the ultimate source of all, including this universe, which is then prefigured in Intellect and transmitted through Soul to become manifest as our physical universe. Matter, which receives imperfectly this expression, is conceived not as an independently existing counter-principle, a dangerously dualist notion, but is in a sense itself a product of the One, a kind of non-being that, while being nothing specific in itself, nevertheless is not simply not there.

But this procession from an ultimate principle is balanced by a return movement at each level of reality that fully constitutes itself only when it turns back in contemplation of its producer. And so the whole of reality is a dynamic movement of procession and return, except for matter, which has no life of its own to make this return; it is inert. This movement of return, which may be traced back to the force of "love" in Plato or Aristotle's final cause, is characterized by Plotinus as a cognitive activity, a form of contemplation, weaker at each successive level, from Intellect through discursive reasoning to the merest image of rational order as expressed in the objects of the physical universe.

The human individual mirrors this structure to which we are all related at each level. For each of us has a body and soul, an intellect, and even something within us that relates to the One. While it is the nature of soul to give life to body, the higher aspect of our soul also has aspirations toward intellect, the true self, and even beyond. This urge to return corresponds to the cosmic movement of return. But the tension between soul's natural duty to body and its origins in the intelligible can be, for the individual, a source of fracture and alienation in which the soul becomes over-involved and overwhelmed by the body and so estranged from its true self. Plotinus encourages us to make the return or ascent, but at the same time attempts to resolve the conflict of duties by reconciling the two-fold nature of soul as life-giving and contemplative.

This is the general framework within which important traditional philosophical issues are encountered, discussed and resolved, but always in a spirit of inquiry and ongoing debate. Issues are frequently encountered in several different contexts, each angle providing a different insight. The nature of the soul and its relationship to the body is examined at length (IV) using the Aristotelian distinctions of levels of soul (vegetative, growth, sensitive, rational) whilst maintaining the immortal nature of the transcendent soul in Platonic terms. The active nature of the soul in sense-perception is maintained to preserve the principle that incorporeals cannot be affected by corporeal reality. A vigorous discussion (VI.4 and 5) on the general nature of the relationship of incorporeals to body explores in every detail and in great depth the way in which incorporeals act on body. A universe that is the product of design is reconciled with the freedom of the individual. And, not least, the time-bound nature of the physical universe and human reason is grounded in the life of Intellect, which subsists in eternity. Sometimes, however, Plotinus seems to break outside the framework of traditional metaphysics: the nature of matter and the One, each as non-being, though in a different sense, strains the terminology and structure of traditional ontology; and the attempt to reconcile the role of the individual soul within the traditional Platonic distinction of transcendent and immanent reality leads to a novel exploration of the nature of the self, the "I."

It is this restless urge for exploration and inquiry that lends to the treatises of Plotinus their philosophical vitality. Whilst presenting us with a rich and complexly coherent system, he constantly engages us in philosophical inquiry. In this way each treatise presents us with new ideas and fresh challenges. And, for Plotinus, every philosophical engagement is not just a mental exercise but also contributes to the rediscovery of the self and our reintegration with the source of all being, the Platonic aim of "becoming like god."

While Plotinus, like Plato, always wishes to engage his audience to reflect for themselves, his treatises are not easy reading, partly no doubt because his own audience was already familiar with many of his basic ideas and, more importantly, had been exposed in his seminars to critical readings of philosophical texts that have not survived to our day. Another problem is that the treatises do not lay out his thought in a systematic way but take up specific issues, although always the whole system may be discerned in the background. Sometimes, too, the exact flow of thought is difficult to follow because of an often condensed mode of expression.

Because we are convinced that Plotinus has something to say to us today, we have launched this series of translations and commentaries as a means of opening up the text to readers with an interest in grappling with the philosophical issues revealed by an encounter with Plotinus' own words and arguments. Each volume will contain a new translation, careful summaries of the arguments and structure of the treatise, and a philosophical commentary that will aim to throw light on the philosophical meaning and import of the text.

John M. Dillon
Andrew Smith

Abbreviations

Armstrong Armstrong, A. H. 1966–1988. *Plotinus.* Greek Text with English Translation and Introductions. 7 vols. Loeb Classical Library. Cambridge, MA: Harvard University Press. Revised edition of vol. I, 1989.

Aubry Aubry, G. 2004. *Plotin: Traité 53 (I, 1).* Introduction, Translation, Commentary, and Notes. Paris: Cerf.

Denniston Denniston, J. D. 1954. *The Greek Particles.* 2nd edition. Oxford: Clarendon Press.

Goodwin Goodwin, W. W. 1889. *Syntax of the Moods and Tenses of the Greek Verb.* London: Macmillan.

HBT Harder, R., R. Beutler, and W. Theiler. 1956–1971. *Plotins Schriften.* Greek Text with German Translation and Commentary. 12 vols. Hamburg: Meiner.

HS_1 Henry, P. and –Schwyzer. 1951–1973. *Plotini Opera* I–III (editio maior). Paris: Desclée de Brouwer et Cie.

HS_2 Henry, P. and -Schwyzer. 1964–1982. *Plotini Opera* I–III (editio minor, with revised text). Oxford: Clarendon Press. Where HS_1 and HS_2 agree, HS indicates this.

KRS Kirk, G. S., J. E. Raven, and M. Schofield. 1983. *The Presocratic Philosophers*. 2nd edition. Cambridge: Cambridge University Press.

LS Long, A. A. and D. N. Sedley. 1987. *The Hellenistic Philosophers, Volume 1: Translation of the Principal Sources, with Philosophical Commentary*. Cambridge: Cambridge University Press.

LSJ Liddell, H. G. and R. Scott, eds. *A Greek–English Lexicon*. 1940. 9th edition, revised by H. S. Jones. Oxford: Clarendon Press.

SP Sleeman, J. H. and G. Pollet. 1980. *Lexicon Plotinianum*. Leiden: Brill and Leuven: Leuven University Press.

SVF Von Arnim, H., ed.1905–1924. *Stoicorum Veterum Fragmenta*. Leipzig: Teubner.

Tornau Tornau, C. 2011. *Plotin: Ausgewählte Schriften*. Translation and Commentary. Stuttgart: Reclam.

VP *Vita Plotini* = Porphyry's *Life of Plotinus*, included in HS_1, HS_2, and in the translations of MacKenna and Armstrong.

Preface and Acknowledgments

I SHOULD LIKE TO THANK John Dillon and Andrew Smith for their invitation to contribute to this series, and for their helpful criticism, which has led to improvements in both the translation and commentary. Recent translations of I.1, and the commentaries or notes that accompany them, have been a stimulus and a challenge: my greatest debts are to Gwenaëlle Aubry and Christian Tornau, but I have also learnt much from Carlo Marzolo and Jean–François Pradeau. More generally, A. H. Armstrong's Loeb translation has been regularly and profitably consulted, and often cited. Other specific debts will be evident from the commentary. The new Clarendon Aristotle volume on the *De Anima* by Christopher Shields has been enormously valuable. At a late stage, David Dusenbury read a complete draft and made several valuable comments.

My wife Ursula has, as ever, been patient, supportive, and critical throughout.

I dedicate the book to a friend of over fifty years, and a scholar whose work has transformed our understanding of classical and late antiquity.

At Parmenides Publishing Gale Carr has been a model of tact and persuasiveness in guiding this book toward completion, and Eliza Tutellier has been the most vigilant of editors: it was a pleasure to work with them.

Introduction to the Treatise

1. The place of I.1 in Plotinus' writings

I.1 was one of the four last treatises sent by Plotinus to Porphyry, his former student and future editor (VP 6, 16–25). Plotinus, seriously ill, had left Rome in 269 for Campania: he died there in 270. I.1 is thus his final treatment of several of his key themes. Porphyry considered that the last nine treatises completed in 269–270 "were written when his (Plotinus') power was already failing, and this is more apparent in the last four than in the five which precede them" (VP 6, 34–37, trans. Armstrong). While it is true that the argument of I.1 is highly condensed, even by Plotinus' standards, and the style strikingly elliptic, there is no sign of any weakening of his analytical powers or philosophical discernment in the treatise. And in general, the last nine treatises contain some of his fundamental essays, on happiness (I.4), on evil (I.8), and (anticipating themes of I.1) on our reasoning soul's relation with Intellect, and with the One or Good (V.3). There are recurring themes in this last sequence: the body-soul relation, the "we" or self, moral responsibility, providence, astrology, and philosophical detachment. There are also signs of forward planning by Plotinus. In II.3 [52], the treatise immediately preceding I.1, he—exceptionally for him—announces the themes of I.1, as follows: "But what the mixed is and what the unmixed, and what the separated is and what the unseparated, when the soul is in the body, and in general what the living thing is, are questions which we must enquire into afterwards, taking a different starting point; for not everyone holds the same opinion on this subject" (II.3.16, 1–4, trans. Armstrong, modified). The implications of this text will become clear in Section 3 below.

2. The choice of I.1 as the opening treatise of Porphyry's edition: the philosophical uses of the Delphic precept

Porphyry says that he placed "mainly ethical" treatises in the first *Ennead* of his edition (VP 24, 16–17). In this respect I.1 is a suitable candidate, for the chiefly psychological themes of its opening chapters lead to discussions of ethical issues in the second part of the treatise. Porphyry also says that he gave first place in each *Ennead* to "less difficult problems" (VP 24, 15–16). But if he envisaged readers beginning with I.1, as he presumably did, then his choice of what is generally recognized as one of Plotinus' more demanding treatises—often allusive, technical, and difficult—makes considerable demands on the reader. For this reason it has been generally assumed that the specific themes of I.1, rather than its style, made it, in Porphyry's view, a suitable opening essay. The overriding concern of Plotinus in I.1 is to describe the human body-soul relation in its temporal dimension, and this involves discussion of how we perceive, how we experience the affections, the relation between our temporal reasoning selves and our higher intuitive intellect, and above all, an attempt to answer the question "what are we?"—the nature of the self or "we" and its relation to consciousness.

These issues are presented in I.1 as the necessary prelude to ethical questions. They can also be understood as part of a tradition of philosophical reactions to the precept inscribed at the temple front of Apollo's oracle shrine at Delphi (and variously attributed to one of the Seven Sages or others): "Know Thyself."[1] Plotinus does not refer explicitly to the Delphic precept in I.1. Elsewhere he cites it, saying that it applies "to those who because of their selves' multiplicity have the business of counting themselves up and learning that they do not know all of the number and kind of things they are, or do not know any one of them, not what their ruling principle is or by what they are themselves" (VI.7.41, 22–25, trans. Armstrong).

1 See Pausanias 10.24.1; O'Daly 1973, 7–19; Courcelle 1974, 11–292.

Although the insistence on the need for a multiple being to have self-knowledge is characteristically Plotinian, this passage has unmistakable echoes of the Platonic dialogue *Alcibiades* 130–133, where knowing what it is to be human is linked to identification of man's ruling principle as the soul, and where the Delphic precept is interpreted as enjoining us to know our souls, and identifying what is best in soul, namely where knowing and understanding occur. Echoes of the *Alcibiades* are also found in I.1.[2]

The *Alcibiades* is not universally considered to be a genuine dialogue of Plato's, but it was included in ancient lists and editions of his works, and Plotinus would not have questioned its authenticity.[3] The short introduction to Plato's dialogues (the *Eisagōgē*) transmitted as a work of Albinus (and so datable to the mid-second century CE) recommends the *Alcibiades* as the Platonic work that a student should first read, "with a view to turning and returning <toward oneself>" (149, 35–36 Hermann).[4] The later Neoplatonists of the fifth and sixth centuries regularly made the *Alcibiades* the starting-point of philosophical studies, and some of them—Olympiodorus, Proclus—wrote commentaries on it.[5]

2 See Commentary 1, 2–4; 3, 2–5.

3 See Denyer 2001 and Velásquez 2013: both argue for its authenticity.

4 For the text see Festugière 1969, 282 with n15.

5 See Festugière 1969; Renaud and Tarrant 2015.

Independently of explicit references to the *Alcibiades*, the identification of self-knowledge as the first topic to be investigated is a philosophical commonplace. It builds on popular injunctions to know oneself, often in the sense of knowing and accepting one's human limitations.[6] There are allusions to the Delphic precept in the Platonic dialogues apart from the *Alcibiades*, of which the most interesting is *Phaedrus* 229e, where Socrates is made to say, "I am not yet capable, in accordance with the Delphic inscription, of 'knowing myself'; it therefore seems absurd to me that while I am still ignorant of this subject I should inquire into things which do not belong to me" (trans. Rowe). Aristotle, in his early dialogue *On Philosophy* asserts that the Delphic precept was the starting point of Socrates' philosophizing (fr. 1 Ross). Xenophon also bases his practical concept of moral self-knowledge on the Delphic inscription (*Memorabilia* IV.2.24–36). The topic (Delphic precept, self-knowledge as knowledge of one's soul) is found in Cicero (*Tusculan Disputations* I.22.52). The Aristotelian philosopher Alexander of Aphrodisias (early third century CE), whose works were read in Plotinus' circle (VP 14, 13), begins his *On the Soul* (*De Anima*) with a citation of the Delphic precept, interpreting its injunction to achieve self-knowledge as knowledge of the substance and powers of our soul, the soul of a body that

6 See Dover 1974, 269; Courcelle 1974, 12–14.

is subject to birth and corruption (*On the Soul* 1.2–2.4). Porphyry himself wrote a work *On "Know Thyself"* of which fragments survive (Porphyry, frs. 272–275 Smith), and which, following Plotinus, distinguished between the self-knowledge of the inner and the outer man.

Porphyry evidently situated I.1 in this tradition of philosophical interpretation of the Delphic "Know Thyself" precept, understood to postulate the necessity of starting philosophy with an investigation of what we really are—the attempt to acquire self-knowledge. He will, then, have found it appropriate to launch readers of Plotinus into this treatise, despite its frequent difficulty and technicality.

3. Arguments and themes of the treatise

The treatise opens with a series of questions to be treated. This sets the tone: much of the argument that follows is aporetic, raising difficulties and showing that they cannot easily be solved. Chapters 1–6 are predominantly devoted to examining problems related to the body-soul relation, especially the questions of how soul is present in body, and how we have sense-perceptions and experience affections. Hypotheses are proposed by Plotinus, some of which are rejected upon closer examination, others are retained for subsequent development. But if the remaining chapters (7–13) are constructive and present elements of a theory, they also signal and discuss further problems.

The overall theme of the treatise is the human soul, its nature and its activities. Plotinus deals with this theme in several earlier treatises, notably the early IV.7 [2] and IV.8 [6], the central treatise IV.3–5 [27–29], and the complex VI.4–5 [22–23] and III.6 [26].[7] I.1 provides a final examination by Plotinus of several key issues in psychology and—inevitably for a Platonist—the related area of ethics. His concept of soul in its broad outlines is consistent throughout these earlier treatises, and I.1 is no exception. We find here the characteristic view that souls descend into bodies from the higher level of Intellect, but that this descent is, from one perspective, not total, and, from another perspective, no descent at all, but that soul remains in the higher intelligible sphere, and a trace of it is projected into bodies. We find also the insistence that soul is not affected by embodiment. It is precisely this insistence that leads to the questions with which the treatise opens: if the soul is impassive, how can we experience affections and receive sense-perceptions, processes that appear to presuppose a corresponding activity of soul? The view that living organisms are initially formed by the world-soul, before the specific trace of the individual soul enters

7 See the commentaries by Dillon and Blumenthal 2015 and Gurtler 2015 on IV.3–5; by Fleet 1996, 2016, 2012 on III.6, IV.7, and IV.8 respectively. On Plotinus' psychology in general see Blumenthal 1971; Caluori 2015 (here 153–171 discussion of I.1). On I.1 and related Plotinus texts see Emilsson 2017, 228–295.

them, is also alluded to.[8] The concept of perception that involves both the transmission of sensations to the soul, and reasoning soul's cognition of these, is advanced here as well as in the earlier treatises, as is Plotinus' insistence that this cognitive aspect of perception is made possible by reasoning soul's access to the Forms that constitute Intellect.[9] But if there is strong continuity between I.1 and the earlier treatises on these cardinal themes, there is also greater precision in several details of Plotinus' views on the soul-body relation. His application of Plato's concept of the "living thing" (*zō(i)on*)—the term is in the title of the treatise—to the entity composed of body and soul-trace, and his location of the affections in this entity, clarifies this aspect of his theory.[10] The detailed restatement of his concept of perception highlights the strengths as well as the problems of the concept.[11] In addition, he integrates these views into his account of the "we" or self in a more explicit and comprehensive way than previously.

8 See Commentary 11, 13–15.

9 Plotinus on perception: Emilsson 1988; Blumenthal 1971, 67–79.

10 The key terms used by Plotinus, with the translations given in the present work, are: *zô(i)on* ("living thing"), *koinon* ("common entity"), *sunamphoteron* ("combination"), *suntheton* ("composite"). See Commentary 5, 1–2.

11 See Commentary 7, 6–16.

A concept of the "we" or self is delineated in some of Plotinus' earlier treatises.[12] The concept may have antecedents in Greek philosophy, but Plotinus' application and development of it are original, and I.1 clarifies his views in a number of important ways.[13] He locates the temporal self in the reasoning soul, but does not confine the self to there, recognizing that "we" are also the entity composed of soul and body-trace and what this entity experiences, and that our unmediated access to Intellect and the Forms makes Intellect a part of us also. He refines the distinction between the "we" and what is, properly speaking, "ours." What emerges is a concept of the self that he can variously describe as "double" or even "multiple." This plurality in the self is accounted for by Plotinus through the related concept of consciousness. What "we" perceive or know or experience is what we are consciously aware of, and this periodic conscious focus is possible because of our continuous unconscious possession of latent capacities, energies, and knowledge. To talk of the self or "we" is not to refer to a faculty (in the sense that intellect and soul are faculties), but to a range of psychological and intellectual processes or activities that we can realize.

---

12 See above all III.4, IV.4.5 and 18, V.1.1 and 12, V.3.2–5, VI.4.14, VI.5.7, VI.7.4–7.

13 See Sorabji 2006, a broad historical survey and analysis. Specifically on Plotinus: O'Daly 1973; Remes 2007; Tornau 2009.

Remarkable as this concept of the self is—and the bland "man" (*anthrōpos*) of the title of the treatise does not prepare us for it—it is important to realize what Plotinus' theory is not. It does not involve personal introspection for its own sake of our individual psyche, or its experiences or memories.[14] Plotinus is not Proust. If, as has been suggested in the preceding section, Plotinus is responding philosophically to the Delphic precept to know ourselves, his self-diagnosis focuses on the characteristics that make us human, rather than on those that make us what we are individually. He is, however, interested in issues relating to our individuality, for example, in whether our souls can, after death, have memories of our prior temporal lives.[15] Also, understanding what we are is, of course, a process made possible by individual cognitive effort, and personal realization through philosophy of our true potential. However, the self we discover is one that we have in common with all other humans, and philosophy should enable us to transcend the temporal self.

I.1 is beyond doubt a treatise in the Platonist mode, intent upon identifying the immortal element in us, the soul, that is separate from body, and speculating about the fate of this element after death. Even in its dealings with the body, the Plotinian soul betrays the influence of Plato.

14 See Stern-Gillet 2007, especially 151–161.

15 See IV.3.24–IV.4.5: commentary in Dillon and Blumenthal 2015, 277–337.

But a striking feature of the treatise is the use throughout of Aristotle (and possibly also of the third century CE Aristotelian philosopher Alexander of Aphrodisias).[16] When, as here, Plotinus enters into the details of empirical psychology, Aristotle's theory of soul, above all in the *De Anima*, provides, not just a terminology, but arguments and insights that help to articulate both the difficulties and the proposed solutions. Aristotle's concept of soul, inextricably linked to the body, cannot become Plotinus' concept, but Plotinus (4, 24–25) can use the best-known Aristotelian definition of soul as a description of the . . . body!

The relation of soul, particularly of reasoning or intellectual soul, to Intellect has been identified above as a theme of the treatise, briefly but tellingly introduced at key moments of the argument. But the characteristic Plotinian concept of the three levels of true being, the hypostases, plays only a minor role in the single reference to the "God" (the highest level, the One or Good), and soul's third-level status in this hierarchy (8, 8–10). This lack of detail should not surprise us. Both in the preceding treatise, where he announces the themes of I.1 (II.3.16, 1–4, quoted in section 1 above) and in the table of contents of the first chapter of the treatise, Plotinus establishes firmly his parameters. He will deal above all with the complex

16 On Aristotle and Plotinus see Blumenthal 1976; Igal 1979. Aristotle and Neoplatonism: Blumenthal 1996.

and controversial topics of what is mixed and unmixed, separate and unseparated, in the body-soul relation and in our activities and powers in our empirical, temporal existence. That he adds to this some glimpses into the possible fate of our souls and soul-traces after death is, Platonically speaking, no surprise.

4. The translation and commentary

I.1 is written in a particularly condensed style, with much ellipsis. To be intelligible, an English translation must supply words not in the original Greek. Where the choice of the words to be supplied is obvious, I have included them tacitly. Where this is not the case, I have inserted the supplied words in angle brackets. Despite, or perhaps because of, its compactness, parts of the treatise give the impression of a lively, informal conversational style, whether in dialogue or monologue. I have tried to convey this informality in the translation, with special attention to the characteristically Greek use of particles and connectives by Plotinus. These often guide and elucidate the course of the argument. Where appropriate, the commentary draws attention to these. I have attempted to preserve terminological consistency throughout. I translate *zō(i) on* as "living thing," rather than the commoner "living being," to avoid the distracting connotations of "being." In translating *aisthēsis* and related terms throughout I have used "perception," "perceive," etc., except where

Plotinus is referring unmistakably to sensation as opposed to perception. In transliterations of Greek words, I have indicated iota subscript by iota adscript in parentheses, as follows: *psuchē(i)*.

Note on the Greek Text

LINE NUMBERS IN THE TRANSLATION are approximate and do not always match the original Greek text. Since the commentary follows the sequence of the English translation, there may sometimes be a slight discrepancy in the ordering.

The Greek text adopted is that of the Oxford edition, that is, the *editio minor* (for comparison between readings in HS_1 and HS_2 see vol. 3, xiii–xiv). Deviations from the text are noted in the commentary.

Each *Ennead* is referred to by Roman numerals, followed by the number of the treatise, the chapter of the treatise, and, finally, separated by a comma, the line number or numbers, for example, VI.8.8, 24–27, that is, *Ennead* VI, treatise number 8, Chapter 8, lines 24–27.

It is customary to add the chronological number given by Porphyry in his *Life of Plotinus* (*Vita Plotini*), so that, for example, VI.8 is designated VI.8 [39], that is, *Ennead* VI.8 is 39th in the chronological order. So we adopt the convention as follows: either VI.8.8, 1–5 (where the chronological number is not given) or VI.8 [39] 8, 1–5 (where it is given).

In this series the chronological number is given only in the Introduction and in other places where it may be of significance for understanding the chronological presentation of Plotinus' philosophical stance. The following chart indicates the chronological order.

Chronological Order of the *Enneads*

Enn.		*Enn.*		*Enn.*		*Enn.*		*Enn.*		*Enn.*	
I.1	**53**	II.1	**40**	III.1	**3**	IV.1	**21**	V.1	**10**	VI.1	**42**
I.2	**19**	II.2	**14**	III.2	**47**	IV.2	**4**	V.2	**11**	VI.2	**43**
I.3	**20**	II.3	**52**	III.3	**48**	IV.3	**27**	V.3	**49**	VI.3	**44**
I.4	**46**	II.4	**12**	III.4	**15**	IV.4	**28**	V.4	**7**	VI.4	**22**
I.5	**36**	II.5	**25**	III.5	**50**	IV.5	**29**	V.5	**32**	VI.5	**23**
I.6	**1**	II.6	**17**	III.6	**26**	IV.6	**41**	V.6	**24**	VI.6	**34**
I.7	**54**	II.7	**37**	III.7	**45**	IV.7	**2**	V.7	**18**	VI.7	**38**
I.8	**51**	II.8	**35**	III.8	**30**	IV.8	**6**	V.8	**31**	VI.8	**39**
I.9	**16**	II.9	**33**	III.9	**13**	IV.9	**8**	V.9	**5**	VI.9	**9**

	Enn.		*Enn.*		*Enn.*		*Enn.*		*Enn.*		*Enn.*
1	I.6	**10**	V.1	**19**	I.2	**28**	IV.4	**37**	II.7	**46**	I.4
2	IV.7	**11**	V.2	**20**	I.3	**29**	IV.5	**38**	VI.7	**47**	III.2
3	III.1	**12**	II.4	**21**	IV.1	**30**	III.8	**39**	VI.8	**48**	III.3
4	IV.2	**13**	III.9	**22**	VI.4	**31**	V.8	**40**	II.1	**49**	V.3
5	V.9	**14**	II.2	**23**	VI.5	**32**	V.5	**41**	IV.6	**50**	III.5
6	IV.8	**15**	III.4	**24**	V.6	**33**	II.9	**42**	VI.1	**51**	I.8
7	V.4	**16**	I.9	**25**	II.5	**34**	VI.6	**43**	VI.2	**52**	II.3
8	IV.9	**17**	II.6	**26**	III.6	**35**	II.8	**44**	VI.3	**53**	I.1
9	VI.9	**18**	V.7	**27**	IV.3	**36**	I.5	**45**	III.7	54	I.7

Synopsis

Chapters 1–6: Problems and hypotheses regarding the soul-body relation and connected issues: soul's impassivity, affections, perception.

Chapter 1. The questions to be discussed in the treatise

1–5: What is the subject of the affections? Three hypotheses: it is (a) the soul, or (b) the soul using a body, or (c) something consisting of soul and body. And if (c), it is either (c.1) a mixture, or (c.2) a new fusion formed from the mixture.

5–8: What is the subject of opinions and of reasoning, and of activities in general?

8–11: What is the subject of intuitive thinking? What is the subject that philosophizes?

11–13: What is the subject of sense-perception? An appropriate starting point, for affections are either perceptions or entail perception.

Chapter 2. Hypothesis (a): the soul as subject of affections, perception, opinion, intellection

1–5: If "soul" and its essence ("to be soul") are distinct, soul is composite and can admit affections.

5–13: If "soul" and its essence are the same, soul is an impassive form, with its own characteristic activity, immortal and incorruptible, receptive only of what it has from higher principles (that is, Intellect and the Good/One).

13–25: The impassive soul cannot experience affections, and so cannot fear, or have desires, or want to be mixed with anything else, or experience distress or delight.

25–27: The impassive soul cannot experience sense-perception, if this entails being acted on by some sensory form or affection. Nor cannot it reason or have opinions, inasmuch as these involve sense-perception.

27–30: How can the impassive soul have intellection, or pure (that is, unmixed) pleasure?

Chapter 3. Introduction of the concept of the "living thing." Hypothesis (b): critique of view that soul uses body (instrumentalism). Hypothesis (c): five kinds of mixture distinguished.

1–3: The embodied soul: the term "living thing" (Plato, *Phaedrus* 246c) introduced.

3–11: The instrumentalist theory criticized, using the craftsman-tool analogy: it need not entail soul being affected by bodily processes. But it is difficult to deny that the soul is somehow affected by perception, and by desires arising in it as a result of opinion or belief.

11–17: But how can affections originating in bodily processes be transmitted to a substance of a different kind like soul? Instrumentalism entails a user-used separation.

17–26: Separation (that is, of soul from body) as a philosophical imperative. It assumes a prior mixture of soul and body. Five kinds of possible mixture are identified: (1) blending; (2) soul is "woven through" body (Plato, *Timaeus*); (3) soul is an unseparated form (Aristotle); (4) soul is "a form in contact" (instrumentalism); (5) combines (3) and (4), with some soul faculties separate, and others mixed with body. Separation through philosophy provides an illustration of this duality and how it may be overcome.

Chapter 4. Hypothesis (c), continued: critique of the kinds of mixture listed in Chapter 3.

1–12: Consideration of option (1) of preceding chapter. Assumption of a dualistic soul-body model creates apparently insurmountable difficulties in accounting for interaction, perception, affections.

12–18: Option (2). A soul "woven through" is not necessarily subject to bodily affections: the analogy of light permeating air is alluded to.

18–27: Options (3) and (4) considered. Option (4) is compatible with instrumentalism. Option (3), soul as unseparated from, is considered more fully, using Aristotle's axe comparison: axe and body-soul as substances formed in a specific way to perform their characteristic functions. Aristotle's definition of soul is adapted to introduce the concept of the "combination" (soul-body), capable of experiencing affections common to soul and body. The "living thing" of Chapter 3, 1–3 is proposed as the subject of affections.

Chapter 5. Detailed discussion of the "living thing." Identification of continuing problems relating to body-soul interaction (affections, perception, opinions).

1–2: The "living thing" is either (i) the "so-qualified body," or (ii) the "common entity," or (iii) a distinct entity fused from body and soul (this is option c.2 of Chapter 1, 1–5).

3–7: In options (i)–(iii) soul must be impassive as cause of affections, or, if passive, must be affected in an identical or similar way as the living thing. If similar, then the living thing and the desiring faculty of soul would be affected in different ways by the same desire.

7–8: Discussion of the so-qualified body of option (i) is postponed to Chapter 7, 1–6.

8–16: Option (ii). The combination = common entity: how can it experience affections, such as distress? Is bodily distress somehow transmitted to perception? But perception has not yet been elucidated. Does a judgment or opinion regarding, for example, pain cause a painful change in the body or living thing? And whose is the opinion, soul's or the combination's?

17–21: One can have opinions relating to affections without experiencing the related affection. But if such opinions are independent of affections, how can these affections be common to body and soul?

21–26: Are the various affections experienced by different soul-faculties (desiring, irascible, appetitive)? But if so, they belong to the soul alone. Yet bodily processes seem to accompany or precede desires or appetites.

26–28: But some desires, such as desire for the Good, are the soul's alone.

29–35: Sexual desire highlights the problem of accounting for soul-body interaction. The man desires, but so does the desiring faculty: which one precedes the other? And if the desiring faculty is the initiator, how can it function if the body is not already so disposed?

Chapter 6. A further hypothesis examined and rejected: soul-powers are unaffected, but transmit related capacities to the soul-body entity.

1–7: A new hypothesis. Perhaps soul-powers are not themselves affected, but transmit the capacity to act to the combination. Thus soul, the cause of life, would be impassive, while the combination acts or suffers.

7–10: But it would then follow that life does not belong to the soul, and the power of perception does not perceive.

10–16: But if perception is a bodily movement ending in the soul (see Chapter 5, 9–11), how can the soul not perceive? Perhaps the combination, possessing the capacity to perceive, consciously perceives. But if the soul-power is unaffected, and neither soul nor soul-power are in the combination, how can the combination perceive?

Chapters 7–13: Attempted solutions and further problems: soul-trace and the undescended soul; perception; the multiple "we" and consciousness; moral responsibility and afterlife punishments.

Chapter 7. The soul-body entity, the "combination," perceives, but it has only a trace of the undescended soul. A theory of perception is outlined, involving both sensation and cognition. Introduction of the concept of the "we."

1–6: The combination does perceive, but soul is present to it only in the form of a distinct trace, analogous to light. Together with body, this trace forms the combination, which perceives and has the other affections of the living thing.

6–16: How is it that **we** perceive? "We" = "man," a multiple entity: Intellect is present to us, as well as the other elements of our substance. Sensation produces impressions of sense-objects: these impressions are intelligibles (sensation has a likeness of these), perceived because the soul impassively (and intuitively) knows the Forms in its undescended state ("alone"). Soul, ruling the living thing, derives its discursive reasoning and opinions from this access to the Forms.

16–18: The "we" (see line 6) is first and foremost at the level of this reasoning soul, but Intellect and the Forms are also ours. We are placed above the living thing.

18–24: The living thing ranges from the irrational element of the soul to the rational soul = "the true man," the reasoning "we."

Chapter 8. Our relation to Intellect and the Forms, and to the "god," the highest principle, transcending Intellect. Soul and its images or powers.

1–8: We possess Intellect in common with all who possess it, for it is indivisible; we possess it as our own, because we possess it completely. Similarly, we know the Forms intuitively in Intellect as a unified whole, and discursively and separated in reasoning soul.

8–10: We have the "God" (= the Good or One) supraposed on Intellect.

10–18: We = soul are at the third level of this hierarchy. Exegesis of Plato, *Timaeus* 35a: soul as indivisible and divided, or apparently divided, giving images or traces of itself in bodies (light and mirror images).

18–23: Among these images are the perceptive, reproductive, and vegetative powers of soul, and in general its creative power directed toward what it produces.

Chapter 9. Ethical considerations: fallibility and evil, the common entity, the unaffected reasoning soul.

1–6: The unaffected soul cannot be responsible for evil, which is the concern of the common entity. But if the soul reasons and has opinions/beliefs, which can be false and harmful, how is it guiltless?

6–12: We are multiple beings. Evil things are done when we succumb to irrational affections or evil images; we believe falsities when we do not use our rational judgment. Likewise, perception can be erroneous if what the common entity perceives is not submitted to rational judgment.

12–15: Intellect is, even in contact with our rational soul, essentially separate from it, and so guiltless. Our contact with Intellect in us may be latent or conscious.

15–23: There are distinctions between activities of the common entity, purely bodily conditions, and that which does not require body for its activation, such as reason's judgment in perception. This last, when it is true reasoning of the true soul, is intellection of Forms in Intellect. There is often a likeness between this reasoning and what is externally sensed.

23–26: The soul is unchanging, self-reflexive, stable; turbulent affections in the common entity (which needs more elucidation) are consequences of embodiment.

Chapter 10. Further discussion of the "we" and its double dimension. Intellectual and habitual virtues, in reasoning soul and the common entity respectively.

1–5: But if we are soul, then how can we be free of affections and change? The common entity is ours in our bodily condition, and what affects our body affects us.

5–7: The "we" is double, referring to the inclusion of the "animal" (the living body), or simply to the higher (= reasoning soul).

7–11: The true man (= reasoning soul), pure (i.e., detached) from the body and "separate" even in this life, has the intellectual virtues; at death the soul-trace departs with it.

11–14: The virtues acquired "by habit and practice" (Plato, *Phaedo* 82a–b), as well as the vices, belong to the common entity.

14–15: Some kinds of friendship belong to the common entity, some to the inner man (= true man/soul).

Chapter 11. Children's souls. Consciousness and the reasoning soul as "middle." Animal souls and transmigration.

1–4: In children the composite is primarily active, the reasoning soul minimally so. But the latter is active toward Intellect, and Intellect is active toward us when it reaches the middle part (= reasoning soul).

4–8: But are we not also what is higher than the middle part? Yes, when there is conscious apprehension, directing the middle part to what is higher or lower than it.

8–13: Animals and the living thing. If they have human souls as a consequence of punitive transmigration, the separate human soul is "present" only in their awareness of its embodied image.

13–15: Where animals have no human soul linked to them, they are ensouled by illumination from the world-soul.

Chapter 12. Problems of posthumous judgments, if the soul is faultless. The soul-trace after physical death. Herakles' double survival explained.

1–5: If soul is faultless, how can it receive posthumous rewards and punishments? What to make of (Platonic) accounts of souls in Hades or reincarnated?

6–12: The faultless soul is a simple entity, "soul" and its essence being the same (see Chapter 2, 1–13). A soul that can commit faults must be composite, and this fallible composite entity experiences affections, and, for Plato, undergoes punishment.

12–20: Citation of extracts from Plato, *Republic* 611–612, applied to separation in this life as well as in the afterlife. Death is complete separation from whatever has been "added" to soul.

20–31: Birth involves the addition of the soul-trace: reference to Chapter 7, 1–6. Soul's "descent," and the accompanying generation of the soul-trace, is a faultless decline. Soul abandons this soul-trace (its image) in death, but in the sense that the trace no longer exists if the soul is totally turned toward Intellect.

31–39: Exegesis of Homer, *Odyssey* XI 601–604. Herakles himself is among the gods on account of his good character, but his image is in Hades because his virtue was practical rather than philosophical.

Chapter 13. We philosophize as soul: soul's non-physical movement. Intellect is a part of us, toward which we aspire.

1–5: What faculty philosophizes (see Chapter 1, 9–11), we or soul? We, with soul, that is, as soul. Reasoning soul moves, but not in a physical sense.

5–8: The soul's higher activity is intellectual and so intellection is ours, and Intellect is a part of us and sustains us. We will ascend toward it.

Translation of
Plotinus Ennead *I.1 [53]*

What is the Living Thing? What is Man?

Chapters 1–6: Problems and hypotheses regarding the soul-body relation and connected issues: soul's impassivity, the affections, perception.

1. Pleasures and pains, fears and confidence, desires and aversions, and distress—what might they belong to? For they are either the soul's, or the soul's using a body, or a third thing's consisting of both. And this last again in two ways: for it is either the mixture, or | another different thing resulting from the mixture.

And the same also holds for what comes to be from these affections, both things done and things opined. And so reason and opinion must be investigated, whether they belong to whatever has the affections, or whether in some cases this is so, but in others it is otherwise.

And intellections are also to be considered, how they occur and whose intellections they are, and also, to be sure, this very thing that | enquires: what might it be that makes the investigation and judgment about these matters?

And before these, perception—who does it belong to? It is appropriate to begin from there, since affections are kinds of perceptions or occur not without perception.

2. First, soul must be considered. Is "soul" one thing, and "to be soul" another?[17] For if this is so, the soul is something composite, and there is nothing strange in this case in its admitting these kinds of affections and in their being its affections—if the argument will actually allow this—| and in general having better and worse habits and dispositions.

On the other hand, if "soul" and "to be soul" are identical, the soul would be some kind of form which does not admit any of these activities which it is able to impart to something else, but having in itself an activity native to itself, whatever the argument may reveal this to be. And so it will be | true to call it immortal, if indeed that which is immortal and incorruptible is necessarily impassive, somehow giving from itself to another, but itself receiving nothing from another, except what it has from the things prior to it, from which it is not cut off, and which are superior to it.

17 See Aristotle, *Metaphysics* VII (*Z*) 6, 1031a15–b14; VIII (*H*) 3, 1043a29–b4.

For what might such a thing fear, being unreceptive of everything external? So let that thing | fear which can be acted upon! And so it is not confident. For is confidence proper to those who are not beset by anything fearful? And how can it have desires, which are satisfied through the body when it is emptied and filled, since what is emptied and filled is other than it? And how could it allow of mixture? Surely the substantial is unmixed. And how could it desire the additional introduction | of anything? For in that case it would be striving not to be what it is. And moreover distress is far from it. For how could it be troubled, and over what? For that which is in fact simple in substance is self-sufficient, remaining as it is in its own substance. And is it pleased when something is added, when nothing, not even something good, may accrue to it? For what it is, | it is always.

Moreover, it will not have sense-perceptions, nor do thought or opinion have to do with it. For perception is the reception of a form or again of a bodily affection, and thought and opinion have to do with perception.

On the other hand, concerning intellection, if we are going to allow this to it, we must enquire how it may have to do with it; and again concerning pure pleasure, whether it can be attributed | to it when it is on its own.

3. But now we must consider the soul in the body, either as existing before it or in it; after all, it is from this combination that "the whole is called a living thing."[18]

Now, if it uses the body as a tool, it is not compelled to undergo the affections that come through the body, | just as craftsmen do not undergo what affects their tools.

But perhaps it might necessarily undergo perception, if it must necessarily use the tool when it knows by perception the things that affect it from outside; since in fact to use the eyes is to see. But there are also misfortunes arising from seeing, so that there can be pains and distress and | in general whatever may happen in connection with the whole body; so desires also occur when soul seeks the care of its tool.

But how will the affections from the body reach it? For body will give things from itself to another body, but how can body give to soul? For this is as if, when one thing is affected, a different thing | is affected. For as long as one is the user and the other is what it uses, each is separate. At any rate, whoever grants that the soul is the user separates them.

But before the separation by philosophy, how was it? There was surely a prior mixture. But if there was a prior mixture, it was either some kind of blending, or soul was, as it were, "woven through,"[19] or it was like an |

18 Plato, *Phaedrus* 246c5.

19 Plato, *Timaeus* 36e2.

unseparated form, or a form in contact, like the helmsman, or one <part> operating in one way and the other in another way. I mean, in so far as one part is separate, that is, the using part, and the other somehow mixed with the body, and being on a level with that which it uses, that philosophy may turn this part also toward the using part and | lead the using part away—in so far as there is not absolute necessity—from what it uses, so that it does not always use it, or use it at all.

4. Let us assume then that a mixture has occurred. But if a mixture has occurred, the worse element, the body, will be better, and the other, the soul, worse; the body better by participating in life, the soul worse by participating in death and unreason. Now how could that which has been deprived of life, no matter in what way, | acquire perception as an addition? On the contrary, it would be the body, acquiring life, that would participate in perception and the affections which come from perception. So this body will be what experiences desire—for it will also enjoy what it desires—and it will fear for itself; for it is not going to achieve | its pleasures and it will be subject to destruction. Also, the mode of this mixture must be investigated, to see whether it isn't absolutely impossible that one nature can be mixed with a different <sort of> nature, as if one were to say that a line is mixed with white.

And the "being woven through"[20] does not make the things woven through <each other> affected in the same way, but it is possible that what is woven through is unaffected, and it is possible that soul, | having permeated, in no way suffers the body's affections—just like light—and especially if it is such that it is interwoven through the whole. So it is not because of the fact that it is woven through that it will suffer the body's affections.

But will it be in the body like form in matter? Well, it will in the first place be there as a separate form, seeing as it is a substance, and | this would correspond more to its using <function>. But, if it is like it is for the axe, the shape imposed upon the iron, and if the combination, the axe, does what it does—the iron shaped in this way, but <performing> in accordance with its shape—we should rather attribute to the body all the common affections, but to "a particular sort" of body, "the natural, | organic, having life potentially."[21] For indeed he[22] says that it is absurd "to say that the soul weaves,"[23] so that it is also absurd to say that it desires or grieves; but rather the living thing does so.

20 See note 19.

21 Aristotle, *De Anima* II.1, 412a27–b1.

22 Aristotle.

23 Aristotle, *De Anima* I.4, 408b12–13.

5. But one should say that the living thing is either the "body of a certain sort,"[24] or "the common"[25] entity, or some other third thing that has come into being from both.

But whatever may be the case, either the soul must keep itself impassive, being the cause of this kind of thing in another, or it must share the experience | as well: and, affected, it must either experience the same affection or a similar one—for example, the living thing might desire in one way, the desiring part act or suffer in a different way.

Now the "body of a certain sort"[26] is to be considered later. But the combination—how, for instance, can it be distressed? Is it because the body | is in this particular state and the affection gets through as far as perception, perception ending in the soul? But it is not yet clear how perception occurs. But whenever pain has its origin in opinion and judgment that some evil is present either to oneself or to someone of one's relatives, then does some painful change occur as a result in the body | and in the living thing as a whole? But it is not yet clear whose the opinion is, the soul's or the combination's.

Besides, the opinion about evil <being present> does not involve the affection of distress. For it is in fact possible for the opinion to be present, and in no way to be distressed as well, and again not to be angry, | although one

24 Aristotle, *De Anima* I.4, 412a16–17.

25 Aristotle, *De Anima* I.4, 408b28–29.

26 See note 24.

has the opinion that one is being belittled, and again for appetite not to be aroused, although one has the opinion that it is an appetite for something good. How then are these affections common?

Is it because desire belongs to the desiring faculty, and anger to the irascible faculty, and in general the stretching out toward anything to the appetitive faculty? But in this case they will no longer be common, but the soul's alone—or even the body's alone, | since blood and bile must boil and the body must be in a certain state to arouse appetite, as in the case of sex.

And it should be granted that the desire for the good is, not a common affection, but the soul's, like others also; upon reflection one does not attribute all affections to the common entity.

But when a man longs for sex, it will be | the man that desires, but it will also be the desiring faculty that desires in a different way. How is this? Will the man start the desire, and the desiring faculty follow? But how could the man desire at all, if the desiring faculty had not been moved? So then, the desiring faculty will start. But if the | body is not previously in this particular state, where will it start from?

6. But perhaps it is better to say that, in general, through the presence of the powers, those who have them are the ones that act in accordance with them, but that they

themselves are unmoved, supplying the capacity to act to those who have them. But if this is so, it is possible that, when the living thing is affected, | the cause of life, having given itself to the combination, remains impassive, whereas the affections and activities belong to what has them. But if this is so, life also will belong, not to the soul at all, but to the combination. So the life of the combination will not be that of the soul, and the power of perception | will not perceive, but that which has the power.

But if perception is a movement through the body that ends in the soul, how will the soul not perceive? Well, when the capacity to perceive is present, through its presence the combination will perceive what it perceives. But if the power | is not going to be moved, how will it still be the combination that perceives, if neither soul nor the soul-power are included in it?

Chapters 7–13: Attempted solutions and further problems: soul-trace and the undescended soul; perception; the multiple "we" and consciousness; moral responsibility and afterlife punishments.

7. Right! Suppose that it is the combination that perceives, the soul, constituted as it is, by its presence not giving itself to the combination or to the other component, but making, out of the body, constituted as it is, and some kind of light given by it, the | nature of the living thing,

something distinct, to which are attributed perceiving and all the other affections of the living thing.

But how is it we who perceive? Surely because we are not separated from the living thing, constituted as it is, even if other things of greater worth are present to us, to make up the whole substance of man, which is composed of many elements. But the power of the soul's perception | need not be of sense-objects, but rather a power able to apprehend the impressions produced from sensation in the living thing. For these are already intelligibles. Thus, external sensation is a likeness of this power of the soul, whereas it is in its essence truer, being a contemplation of forms alone, impassively. Moreover, it is from these | forms—from which the soul, alone, already receives leadership over the living thing—that reasonings and opinions and intellections come.

And it is precisely there, above all, that we are situated. The things before these are ours, but we are actually what comes next, placed above, over the living thing.

There will be no impediment to calling the whole "living thing"; as it is mixed both with respect to the lower <components> and | what comes next, the true man, so to speak. But the former are the "lion-like" element and, in short, the "variegated animal";[27] whereas, since man

27 Plato, *Republic* IX, 588c7, 588d3, 590a9–b1.

coincides with the reasoning soul, when we reason, it is *we* who reason, for reasonings are activities of the soul.

8. But how are we in relation to Intellect? By "Intellect" I mean not the state of the soul as one of the things which are from Intellect, but Intellect itself. For to be sure we have this too, above us. We have it either in common, or as our own, or both common to all and our own: common, | because it is indivisible and one and everywhere the same; our own, because each has it as a whole in his primal soul. And so we also have the Forms in two ways, in the soul unrolled, so to speak, and separated, in Intellect all together.[28]

But how do we possess the God? Surely as one being mounted on the intelligible nature and the | essence that is truly essence,[29] and we are third from there, composed, he says, of "the indivisible" above, "and from the <essence> divided in bodies,"[30] which one must conceive of as so divided in bodies that it gives itself to bodily magnitudes whatever the size of each living thing, for it gives itself to the universe too, while being | one; or in the sense that it is imagined to be present to bodies, since it shines into them and makes living things, not out of itself and body,

28 See Anaxagoras, fr. 1.

29 See Numenius, fr. 2, 16.

30 Plato, *Timaeus* 35a1–3.

but remaining itself unchanged and giving images of itself, like a face in many mirrors.

The first image is perception in the common entity; then, following this in turn, everything that is called "another kind | of soul,"[31] each always following the other. It ends with the power of reproduction and that of growth, and in general the power of making something distinct—productive, that is, of something distinct from the soul which makes, while that which makes is turned toward what is produced.

9. So the nature of that soul of ours will be free from the responsibility for all evils that a man does and suffers. These have to do with the living thing, the common entity, and "common" as it has been described. But if opinion and reasoning are proper to the soul, how is it free from error? | For opinion is deceitful and many evils are done because of it.

Now evils are done when we are overcome by what is worse—for we are multiple—by desire or anger or an evil image. And so-called thinking what is false, being an imagining, has not waited for the judgment of the reasoning faculty, but | we have acted, persuaded by what is worse, just as in the case of perception, it happens that

31 Plato, *Timaeus* 69c7.

the common perception sees falsely, before the reasoning faculty passes judgment.

The intellect is either in contact, or not, and thus free from error. Perhaps, though, one should put it as follows: that we are in contact with the intelligible in Intellect, or not. Or rather, with the intelligible in us: | for one can have it and not have it to hand.

So then, we have distinguished between the common activities and the ones peculiar to soul, in that the former are bodily, or cannot exist without body; but what does not require body for its actualization is peculiar to soul; and reasoning, making a judgment on the impressions produced from sensation, is already | seeing forms, and seeing them, so to speak, self-consciously—at any rate, the reasoning, in the proper sense, of the true soul does. For true reasoning is the actualization of intellections and often involves a likeness and community between what is outside and what is within.

So the soul will nonetheless stay calm, concentrated upon itself and in itself. The changes and the | tumult in us arise from what has become attached and, as has been described, from the affections of the common entity, whatever this is.

10. But if we are the soul, and we are affected in this manner, it would be the soul that is affected in this manner, and again it will do what we do. Now we said that the

common entity also is ours, and especially when we have not yet been separated from the body: for what affects our body, | we say too that it affects us.

So the "we" is double, either with the animal included, or what even now is above this: the animal is the body endowed with life. But the true man is other, pure of these things, possessing the virtues in intellection, those, that is, seated in the separating soul itself, separating and separate | while still here. For when it actually withdraws entirely, the soul illuminated by it departs also, following along with it.

But the virtues which are produced, not by reason, but by "habit" and "practice,"[32] belong to the common entity: for the vices also belong to this, since envy and jealousy and pity do.

And what do friendships belong to? Well, some belong | to this, some to the inner man.[33]

11. When we are children, what comes from the composite is active, and little shines upon it from the things above. But when <what is above> is inactive toward us it is active toward what is above it. And it[34] is active toward us when it reaches the middle <part>.

32 Plato, *Republic* VII, 518e1–2.

33 See Plato, *Republic* IX, 589a7–b1.

34 I.e., Intellect.

What? Are we not also what is before this? | But there must be conscious awareness. For we do not always use all that we have, but only when we direct the middle part either toward what is above or toward the opposite, whatever, that is, we are bringing from potentiality or disposition to actuality.

But how does the living thing include the animals? Well, if, as is said, there should be human souls in them | that have done wrong, this, inasmuch as it is separate, does not belong to the animals, but, being present, is not present to them; but their consciousness has an image of the soul that is with the body. So theirs is a body of such a kind made, so to speak, by an image of soul.

But if a human soul has not entered the animal, it is by illumination from the universal soul that this kind of living thing | has come into being.

12. But if the soul is faultless, how are there judgments? Certainly this argument of ours is in disagreement with every argument that asserts that it both commits faults and acts rightly, and undergoes punishment and is in Hades and is reincarnated. Now one may assent to whichever | argument one wishes; and perhaps one can even find out how they are not in conflict.

For the argument granting faultlessness to the soul posited that it is a single altogether simple entity, saying that "soul" and "to be soul" are the same,[35] whereas the argument that grants that it commits faults weaves into and adds to it quite another kind of soul, which has the dreadful passions. | Thus the soul becomes composite and is composed of all its parts, and it is "the composite"[36] that is affected in its entirety and commits faults, and it is this which, for him,[37] undergoes punishment, not the other.

Hence he says, "we have seen" it "like those who see the marine god Glaukos." But "one should chip off" what has been added, | if one wants, he says, "to see its nature and see its love of wisdom, and what it is in contact with, and akin to what" it is what it is.[38] So there is another life and other activities and that which is punished is different. And the withdrawal and the separation are not only from this body but from everything | that has been added.

For indeed the addition is at birth; or rather, birth belongs to the other kind of soul. How birth occurs has been explained, that when soul descends, something else comes into being from it, descending in its decline. So, does it then abandon its image? And how is its decline not a fault? But if the | decline is an illumination directed toward what is below, it is not a fault, any more than a shadow is, but what is illuminated is to blame, for if it

35 See note 17.

36 Plato, *Republic* X, 611b5.

37 Plato.

38 Plato, *Republic* X, 611c7–d1, 611e1–612a4.

did not exist, soul can in no way illuminate. So it is said to descend or decline in that what has been illuminated from it has come to live with it. So it does abandon its image, if that which received it is not close by. And it abandons it, | not in the sense that it[39] is cut off, but in that it is no longer there: it is no longer there, if soul is wholly looking There.

The poet[40] seems to separate this[41] in the case of Herakles, explaining that his image is in Hades, but that he himself is among the gods, constrained as he was by both versions, that he is among the gods, and that he is in Hades:[42] so he divided him. | But perhaps the story might be plausible in the following way: because Herakles had practical virtue and was considered worthy to be a god on account of his fine character, and because he was a practical person and not a thinker—in that case he would be wholly There—he is above and there is still something of him below as well.

13. That which has investigated these matters—is it we or the soul? Well, it is we, but with the soul. In what way, "with the soul"? Is it that it investigated because it has soul? No, rather inasmuch as it is soul. Will it be moved

39 I.e., the image.

40 Homer.

41 I.e., the image.

42 Homer, *Odyssey* XI, 601–604.

then? Well, movement must be granted to it, of such a kind that it is not physical, | but is its life.

And intellection is ours in the sense that the soul is intellectual, and intellection is a superior life, both when the soul intelligizes, and when Intellect directs its activity toward us. For Intellect too is a part of us and toward this we shall ascend.

Commentary

Title

In Porphyry's chronological sequence, the treatise has the title "What is the living thing?" (VP 6, 22). In the systematic list of *Enneads* as ordered by Porphyry the title is, "What is the living thing, What is man?" (VP 24, 18), and this is the title in the table of contents (the *pinax*) in the manuscripts of the *Enneads* (with the usual introductory "Concerning" [*peri tou*]). "Living thing" (or "living being") alludes to Plato, *Phaedrus* 246c5 (*zō(i)on*), quoted in Chapter 3, 2–3 (see Commentary 3, 1–3): the word commonly means "animal," including humans. "Man" (*anthrōpos*) in the second question of the title means "human being."

Chapter 1

The opening chapter sets the scene for the themes to be discussed in the treatise, in a series of explicit and implicit questions. Where are the affections located (Chapters 2–7)? What is the body-soul relation (Chapters 2–7)? Are opinion and reason located in the same faculty as the affections (Chapters 2, 9)? How and in what subject does intellection occur (Chapters 8, 13)? Where is sense-perception located (Chapters 2, 3, 6, 7)? When we philosophize, what is the investigating and judging faculty (Chapter 13)? This brief overture or prelude is equivalent to a table of contents. It pinpoints the main psychological themes of the treatise. The ethical aspects, not apparent here, will become clearer as the argument develops (especially in Chapters 9–12). The question of the self, or "we," comes to the fore from Chapter 7 on, in connection with discussions of the soul-body relation, mind, and ethics. Porphyry, placing this treatise at the head of his edition of Plotinus' writings, emphasizes the role that the series of questions plays in an introduction to philosophy as he conceives it.

1, 1–2 *Pleasures and pains . . . what might they belong to?*: The list of affections is traditional, and the first three named—pleasure, pain, and fear—are among the commonest in earlier philosophical discussions (together with desire or appetite, they are for the Stoics the "generically prior" passions, LS §65A = SVF III 378). Plotinus, following the frequent practice of earlier lists, has pairs of contrasting affections, followed by the more general "distress." HS, followed by other commentators, refer to Plato, *Republic* 429c–d, 430a–b; *Phaedo* 83b; *Timaeus* 69d, and Aristotle, *De Anima* I.4, 408b2–3. Armstrong I, 94n1, refers to Plato, *Laws* 896e–897a. Marzolo 2006, 81 cites one of the fullest lists, Aristotle, *Nicomachean Ethics* II.5, 1105b21–23 ("desire, anger, fear, confidence, envy, joy, love, hatred, longing, jealousy, pity"), and adds as a possible source for Plotinus here Alexander of Aphrodisias, *On the Soul* 12.7–19, where the passions are adduced as evidence that soul's activities cannot occur without bodily movement or change. Pradeau 2010, 202, concurs, but there seems to be no need to privilege the Alexander passage as a specific source here.

The pairing of fear and confidence (*tharros*) here probably follows their juxtaposition in Aristotle as potential extremes of excess or deficiency in relation to the mean, the virtue of courage (*Nicomachean Ethics* II.7, 1107a33–b4; the theme is developed by Aristotle later in the same work, III.6–9). Fear and confidence are also juxtaposed in Chapter 2, 13–16 of our treatise. One term used by Plotinus, "aversions (*apostrophai*)," is unusual in accounts of the affections, and may be of medical origin as a technical term for an excessive or morbid dislike of something (LSJ, *apostrophē* IV cites Aretaeus and Galen). In III.6.3, 1 Plotinus uses the term "avoidances (*allotriōseis*)," and we may assume (see Fleet, 1995, 104–106) that he means by this term affections like fear and distress. Aristotle speaks likewise of avoidance (*phugē*) and pursuit in relation to pleasures (*Nicomachean Ethics* III.4, 1113b1–2; see *De Anima* III.7, 431a7–14).

The plural forms used in the Greek to refer to the first six affections in lines 1–2 may suggest, as later in 10, 14, that the affections are processes or alterations rather than states: see Fleet 1995, 105. The phrase translated as "what might they belong to?" is repeated in various forms throughout the chapter: Plotinus emphatically wants to identify the location of—or subject experiencing—the affections, as well as the other psychological activities or processes referred to in the course of the chapter. To what may they be attributed? The next sentence specifies the three options.

1, 2–4 *For they are either the soul's . . . composed of both*: The options as location of the affections—soul, soul using a body, or a composite of these—echo the *Alcibiades*, where "man" is said to be "soul or body or these two together" (130a9), and where the argument that the soul uses the body is developed (129e–130b: the statement that the soul uses, or rules, or has care of, the body is frequent in Plato, see *Phaedo* 79c, 80a, *Phaedrus* 246b6–7): this argument is discussed in Chapter 3 of the treatise. The *Alcibiades*, assumed to be a genuine Platonic work in antiquity and by many modern scholars (see Denyer 2001 and Velásquez 2013), is likely to have been influential later in the treatise, when Plotinus discusses the question "what are we?" It was the first work studied in the Platonic schools of late antiquity (Festugière 1969; for its influence see Renaud and Tarrant 2015), and Alexander of Aphrodisias begins his treatise *On the Soul* with a reference to the injunction of the Delphic oracle, "Know Thyself," echoing the *Alcibiades* in this respect. This theme is undoubtedly a factor influencing Porphyry in his choice of this treatise as the opening one of his Plotinus edition. But, as Aubry 112–113, points out, Aristotle, *De Anima* I.1, 403a10–12, is also influential. There Aristotle, introducing the question of the soul's essence or substance, asks whether there are affections or activities of soul that are peculiar to it, or if all its affections and activities are common to it and body. This Aristotelian approach will determine Plotinus' analysis in the following chapters, even if his answer to the question will be different from Aristotle's.

1, 4–5 *And this last again . . . resulting from the mixture*: The question whether soul-body might be a mixture (*migma*) or a *tertium quid* reflects (as Aubry 111 observes) the Stoic distinction between a mixture (*krasis*), where the mixed elements retain their particular qualities, or a fusion (*sugchusis*), where they do not. Like the Stoics, but for different reasons (for the Stoics soul is something bodily), Plotinus will argue for a kind of mixture rather than fusion.

1, 5–8 *And the same also holds . . . with others it is otherwise*: Experiencing affections may be a prelude to action or belief: these, and opinion and reason in general, may have the same subject as the affections, or some opinions and acts of reasoning may do so, while others do not. Plotinus is expressing himself as generally and neutrally as possible throughout this opening chapter. He does not want to preempt the discussion to come. "Reason" (*dianoia*) in line 7 is the discursive thinking that we normally engage in: like opinion, it can be true or false. So the relation of opinion and reason to the affections is problematic. Plotinus returns to this problem, and offers a solution, in Chapter 9, 4–12 (see Commentary 9, 1–6 and 6–12). The term for affections in line 6, *pathēmata*, seems to have the same meaning as *pathē* here, as it does in Aristotle, but elsewhere, as in III.6.1–5, it refers to perceptive impressions or experiences (see Fleet 1995, 72–74). But Plotinus seems nonetheless to echo here the discussion initiated in III.6.1, 1–7 of the links between affections, perception, activity, and judgment.

1, 8–11 *And intellections are also to be considered . . . judgment about these matters?*: By "intellections (*noēseis*)" Plotinus means the intuitive thinking characteristic of intellect (*nous*), which we have the potential of activating in us. Enquiring into the subject of our intellections is naturally related to enquiring into the subject that philosophizes, but Plotinus' subsequent discussion will distinguish between the two.

1, 11–13 *And beforehand . . . not without perception*: Sense-perception is an appropriate starting point of the investigation, since the affections—the first topic mentioned by Plotinus at the beginning of the chapter—are either perceptions or presuppose perception. Plotinus is once again keeping his options open here. In fact, he has argued in the earlier treatise III.6 [26], 1 that perceptions and affections must be distinguished from one another. And he will actually start in the next chapter with discussion of the nature of soul in general, before considering perception. We should bear in mind that Plotinus' term for the latter—*aisthēsis*—has different meanings. Sometimes it means "sensation," but I have preferred to translate it throughout as "perception" unless it clearly refers to sensation as opposed to perception (as at 7, 10 and 12). And, like the related verb *aisthanesthai* (which occurs here in line 11), it can also refer to the faculty of perception, to mental perception (e.g., I.4.9, 10 and 15), or to conscious apprehension (see Commentary 11, 4–8). Here, as often in other respects, Plotinus' vocabulary is influenced by Aristotle's usage (for *aisthēsis* in the latter see Shields 2016, 391).

Chapter 2

This chapter addresses an aspect of the second question of the opening chapter: is the soul something composite or not? It does not answer the question (though it is obvious what Plotinus' answer would be), but considers the implications of the alternatives. The affections are reintroduced, reflecting the opening sentence of Chapter 1, in a lively series of rhetorical questions and assertions. Aristotle's influence is evident in the choice of terminology and the manner in which the question of the soul's substance is approached. Toward the end of the chapter further issues are briefly raised: perception, intellection, "pure" pleasure. Overall, Chapter 2 pinpoints themes that will be discussed more thoroughly in the following chapters.

2, 1–2 *First soul must be considered. Is "soul" one thing, and "to be soul" another?*: The distinction between "soul" and "to be soul" is made without explanation. It is a reference to Aristotle, but a highly allusive one. Plotinus' intentions become clearer when the detail of the Aristotelian texts is considered. Here are the two relevant passages (commentary in Ross 1924, 2.175–178 and 230–231; Bostock 1994, 103–111 and 261–262; brief and helpful discussion of the issues in Ackrill 1981, 122–128):

(a) We must not forget that sometimes it is not clear whether a word signifies the composite substance (*tēn suntheton ousian*), or the actuality (*energeian*) or shape (*morphēn*), for example, whether "house" is a sign for the composite thing (*sēmeion tou koinou*), "a shelter consisting of bricks and stones placed thus," or for the actuality or form (*eidous*), "a shelter". . . and whether "an animal" (*zō(i)on*) means a soul in a body or a soul. For the latter is the substance (*ousia*) or actuality of a certain body; but "animal" might be applied to both, not that both are definable by one formula but because they both refer to the same thing . . . what it is to be (*to ti ēn einai*) clearly attaches to the form (*eidei*) and the substance (*energeia(i)*). For "soul" and "to be soul" (*psuchē(i) einai*) are the same, but to be man and man are not the same, unless the soul too is to be called man. (Aristotle, *Metaphysics* VIII (*H*).3, 1043a29–b4, trans. Ross, modified and with omissions).

(b) We must consider whether each thing and what it is to be (*to ti ēn einai*) for it are the same or different. This is of some use for the investigation of substance (*ousia*); for each thing is thought to be not different from its substance, and what it is to be for a thing is said to be the substance of each thing. Now in the case of things which are spoken of incidentally the two would be generally thought to be different: for instance, "a pale man" would be thought to be be different from "to be a pale man." For if they were the same, to be a man and to be a pale man would also be the same . . . But in the case of things spoken of in their own right, are they necessarily the same as what it is to be for them? For example, if there are some substances which have no other substances or natures (*phuseis*) prior to them—substances such as some assert the Forms to be? . . . The good . . . must be the same as to be good (*to agathō(i) einai*), and the beautiful the same as to be beautiful, and so with all things which are not spoken of in relation to something else but are spoken of their own right and are primary (Aristotle, *Metaphysics* VII (Z).6, 1031a15–22, 1031a28–31, 1031b11–14, trans. Ross, modified).

It is important to realize that Plotinus' use of these passages is at once selective and skilful. Consider the two passages before turning to Plotinus' exploitation of them.

In (a) the issue is: what does a name refer to? "House" and "animal" can refer to the composite material entity, or to the actuality or form, that is, to what Aristotle calls "what it is to be," the essence, that which makes something what it is. Now soul for Aristotle is the actuality or substance of a body: in *De Anima* II.1, 412a19–20 he states that soul is substance, inasmuch as it is the form of a natural body. In the case of "house" or "man," where the name can refer either to the composite entity or to the actuality or substance (in the case of "man" it could refer to man's soul as actuality or substance), there is no necessary coincidence of reference and definition. But in the case of "soul" there is such necessary coincidence. In Aristotle's standard terminology "soul," the referent, and "to be soul," the essence, are the same. Here Aristotle uses the abbreviated phrase "to be soul" (with "soul" a predicative dative in the Greek) to refer to the essence: the full phrase is "what it is to be soul" (*to ti ēn einai psuchē(i)*). On the Greek idiom of the phrase see Goodwin §781; Barnes 1993, 174.

In (b) above, a passage earlier in the *Metaphysics* that complements the argument of (a), Aristotle also considers the relation of a thing to its essence. A thing's substance and its essence ("what it is to be for it") would seem to be the same. A non-substantial or accidental predication ("things spoken of incidentally"), such as "pale" of "man" would not refer to the man's essence. But self-subsistent things ("things spoken of in their own right") must be one with their essence. The examples Aristotle goes on to give, of the Platonic Ideas or Forms, are of things whose real existence he does not believe in; but, so the argument goes, if they were to exist they would be one with their essence ("what it is to be for them"). Aristotle in this passage uses the full phrase referred to above ("what it is to be for a thing"), as well as the abbreviated phrase form "to be (a pale) man/good/beautiful").

To return to Plotinus. A passage in an earlier treatise shows that he has absorbed Aristotle's argument. In VI.2 [43] he argues that to say that the soul exists is not the same as saying that a stone exists. Yet "in the case of the stone also, existing for the stone is not just being but being a stone (*to lithō(i) einai*); so here, existing for soul (*to einai psuchē(i)*) has being soul along with being." Plotinus asserts that being is not something that completes the soul's substance (one might add that it does not complete the stone's substance either), that soul is a "particular being (*ti on*) but not in the way that a man is pale, but only and simply like a particular substance (*hōs tis ousia monon*) . . . it does not have what it has from outside its substance" (VI.2.5, 19–26, with omissions, trans. Armstrong, modified). Here, as in the Aristotle passages cited above, one notes the distinction between substantial/essential and non-substantial predication. Plotinus' argument might seem to leave the asserted difference between being soul and being a stone unexplained, but in the next chapter of VI.2 he elucidates: the substance that soul has, not from outside but within, is the life that is one with its being, by contrast with the stone's lack of life (VI.2, 6). See Corrigan 1996, 330–390 on Aristotelian and Plotinian substance (*ousia*), and 317–319 on VI.2, 4–6; on substantial and non-substantial predications see Aristotle, *Posterior Analytics* I.22, 82b37–84b2, with Barnes 1993, 174–181.

What is revealing about Plotinus' argument is his use of Aristotle, despite his different concept of the soul. For Aristotle, soul is the substance or actuality of a particular body (with the proviso that mind might perhaps exist separately from body). Plotinus, on the other hand, conceives of soul as something that exists independently of body, a concept of soul that, at least in this respect, is found in Plato (*Phaedo* 64c–67b). In earlier treatises Plotinus has argued for the soul's immateriality, simplicity, immortality, and impassivity (III.6.1–5; IV.7). He is not going to depart from this position here, even if he will, in subsequent chapters, clarify his concept of the soul-body relation. Yet the line of argument found here and in VI.2, 5–6 is underwritten by Aristotelian method, and Aristotelian discourse about substance, predication, essence, composite entities, "animal," and "man." It is no accident that the chapter is introduced by Aristotle's way of asking the question: what makes the soul what it is?

2, 2–5 *For if this is so . . . habits and dispositions*: Plotinus builds on his brief allusion to Aristotle by arguing that if soul and its essence are distinct, soul must be a composite. He does not spell out why this is so, expecting us to infer from Aristotle's argument that in this case "soul" must refer to a composite entity, just as "house" or "animal" or "man" can refer to composite entities, when we are not referring to their actuality or form or essence. He can do this, because he accepts Aristotle's assertion that to refer to "soul" is unambiguous, as it is always a reference to soul's substance *qua* form and actuality. Plotinus dwells only briefly on the implications of a hypothetical distinction between soul and its essence or definition. It would entail that soul has passions and can be in better and worse moral states, and can behave better or worse. It would therefore entail soul's fallibility as moral subject. The phrase "if the argument (*logos*) will actually allow this" (line 4) must refer to the argument that soul and its essence are distinguishable. This hypothesis of an optional concept of soul is maintained throughout the chapter, as is indicated by the reference a few lines later to the argument (*logos*, 9) for the alternative.

2, 5–13 *On the other hand . . . which are superior to it*: Plotinus' presentation of the implications of the alternative option, that "soul" and "to be soul" are the same, is given considerably more space; after all, it is his preferred view. But he maintains it as a hypothesis, generally speaking if not always (he repeatedly slides into assertion), for the rest of the chapter. Although he agrees with Aristotle that "soul" and "to be soul" are the same, his survey of the implications reveals a radically different concept of soul. He may call soul a form (*eidos*), as Aristotle does, but it is a form that is not necessarily embodied, it has its own innate activity (*energeia*), it does not admit of affections or varying moral habits or conditions. Plotinus is anticipating the argument of later chapters that will clarify these assertions. His claim that soul's immortality and incorruptibility entail its impassivity does not follow from what he has just been arguing: if anything, the converse would seem to be the case (Aubry 124). In VI.8.14, 4–7, another passage where Aristotle's analysis is alluded to, he argues more correctly from soul's simple and self-subsistent ("not predicated of something else") nature that "soul" and "to be soul" are the same. In the present chapter he adds that soul's impassivity does not preclude it from "giving from itself to another" (l. 11), another assertion that requires later elucidation, but which Plotinus' readers and members of his school will recognize as an invocation of what has been called his "principle of undiminished giving," where the giver is not diminished in any way by giving (see, e.g., V.1.6, V.2.1, V.4.2). Likewise, the reference that follows to "things prior to" the soul invokes the hierarchy of principles (the so-called hypostases), in which Intellect (*nous*) and the Good are superior to soul. These shorthand references complicate the picture at this stage of the argument, but they are also signposts to later themes.

2, 13–25 *For what might such a thing fear . . . what it is, it is always*: There is a change of style and tone in this section. The theme of the affections returns, and several of them—fear, confidence, desires, distress, pleasure—are invoked in a series of questions, mainly rhetorical, and vigorous assertions or denials. Particles, adverbs, and a striking verb add drama and a certain colloquial colour: "so!" (*toinun*, 14, 15), "surely" (*ē*, 19), "it would be rushing" (*speudoi*, 20), "in effect" (*ge*, 22). The same point is made throughout the question series: the substance soul cannot be acted upon by impulses or affections. On the juxtaposition of fear and confidence (*tharros*) see Commentary 1, 1–2. Physical desires are described in Platonic terms as processes of bodily depletion and replenishment (Plato, *Timaeus* 64e–65b).

Sometimes Plotinus' ellipsis is extreme: "And how . . . mixture?" (line 16) has been completed (supplying "desire" or "admit" or, in my translation, "allow of") and understood differently by commentators. Most commentators understand "mixture" to refer here to body-soul mixture in general, in an assertion that soul-substance cannot admit (or desire) such mixture. That would express a characteristic Platonist view, and in Plotinus' announcement of the treatise in the immediately preceding II.3.16, 1–4 "what the mixed is and what the unmixed" is the first theme announced, and is, of course, a cardinal theme of I.1, referred to as early as 1, 4. But why make this general point here, in the specific context of desires? The interpretation given by Tornau 312 (with 426n6) supplies the verb "desire," and understands "mixture" (*mixis*) to refer to "sexual intercourse," as in VP 15, 9 and, one might add, III.5.1, 28 and 38 (a common meaning, see LSJ, *mixis* II). Tornau's interpretation is tempting, for sexual desires are an obvious inclusion in any survey of desires, and accounting for them is problematic for Plotinus, as the later discussion in 5, 24–35 demonstrates. There, however, he refers unambiguously to sex (*aphrodisia*).

The notion of soul as a simple substance (*to ge haploun en ousia(i)*, 22) adds a crucial element to the description of the immortal, incorruptible, impassive soul of lines 10–11. The use of *ousiōdes* and *ousia*, differently rendered by earlier translators as "substantial, substance" and "essential, essence," reminds us that these terms, in Aristotle as here in

Plotinus, are ambiguous. If the former pair is adopted in this translation in lines 19 and 22–23 because Plotinus' seems to be talking about the soul as basic being, it is of course also the case that he is talking about what makes the soul what it is, its essence.

In lines 15–16, "For is confidence . . . who are not beset . . .": the relative clause is a conditional relative with the subjunctive + *an*, and could be translated "if they are never . . ." (Goodwin §532).

2, 25–27 *Moreover, it will not have sense-perceptions . . . have to do with perception*: Plotinus returns briefly to what he called the first question at the end of Chapter 1, sense-perception. He will return to it repeatedly in the following chapters before giving his final account of it in Chapter 7. But each reiteration of the theme brings points of detail to his account. Here he emphasizes that perception is reception of a form (*eidos*): by this he must mean, at this stage of the treatise, a sensible, if non-material, form, as posited by Aristotle, *De Anima*, II.12, 424a17–24. Plotinus adds that perception is also reception of a "bodily affection": this translates Gollwitzer's emendation *kai pathous*; for *ē kai* in the sense of "or again," with possible imitation of Plato, see Denniston 306–307. The manuscripts' reading *apathous*, "of an impassive body," is due to scribal concern about asserting that perception is of a bodily affection. Again, he must mean by "reception . . . of a bodily affection" some kind of non-material sensory quality, but this is not explained at this stage. He is focusing on the argument, implicit here in this series of questions and assertions, that perceptions of this kind would entail the soul's being acted on. Reasoning and opinion are mentioned here again, as in Chapter 1: their link with perception means that they can, it must be implied, be true or false. The soul as invoked in the present chapter is a self-sufficient simple substance in a steady state: it cannot admit the flux of changing thoughts and opinions. The curious reader may (and should) ask: how then does the soul think? What subject is thinking when discursive thought (*dianoia*, 25) occurs? Plotinus will address these questions later in the treatise.

2, 28–30 *On the other hand, concerning intellection . . . when it is on its own*: The reference to intellection (*noēsis*) here simply rephrases the question of Chapter 1, 8–9: there the issue was the subject of intellection, here it is intellection's relation to the soul. As for "pure pleasure," Plotinus does not return to this question in the treatise. He is presumably thinking of the unmixed or true pleasures discussed in Plato's *Philebus* 50e–55c (which interestingly include perceptions of pure colors, geometrical shapes, and single pure sounds or notes or smells: see D. Frede 1993, liii–lviii), perhaps also of the kind of pleasure found in the activation of Intellect in us and in "getting in touch with" and enjoying the Good, the principle of the divine things (and so of all things), as evoked in VI.7.30 (see Aubry 136n11).

The reference in line 30 to the soul being "on its own (*monēn*)" is to its ability to "intelligize," that is, to think independently of body: there is further elucidation in 7, 13–16 of the concept of the soul "alone" contemplating "forms alone" (see Commentary 7, 6–16).

Chapter 3

In the previous chapter Plotinus explored some of the implications of positing an impassive soul. The chief implication is that it becomes difficult to account for activities that seem to presuppose a body-soul relation, and the present chapter is a first attempt to investigate this relation. The concept of the "living thing" (zō(i)on)*, the body-soul entity, is introduced: it will dominate the remainder of the treatise. But the overall tone of the chapter is aporetic, raising questions and identifying problems. These are mostly familiar from the two opening chapters—how to account for perception, for affections—but the perspective has shifted, and the body-soul combination, as well as the separability of soul and body, are now the focus. Plotinus proposes five ways in which soul-body might be said to be a mixture: (1) soul and body are blended, (2) soul is woven through body, (3) soul is an unseparated form, (4) it is a form in contact with body, or (5) it is partly separate and partly mixed with body.*

3, 1–3 *But now . . . "the whole is called a living thing"*: The opening words "But now" (translating *alla gar*, see Denniston 106) announce emphatically a new phase of the argument. Plotinus quotes Plato, *Phaedrus* 246c5 ("the whole, body and soul compacted, is called a living thing"), from a passage in which Plato is discussing the "form" (*idea*, 246a3) of the soul and its embodiment. The word *zō(i)on*, here translated as "living thing," commonly means "animal," including humans. It occurs in the first part of the title of this treatise. The term "living thing," equivalent to the "combination" (*sunamphoteron*) of body and soul-power, has already been used in IV.3.25, 38–42.

3, 3–5 *Now, if it uses the body . . . what affects their tools*: The craftsman-tool analogy used here echoes *Alcibiades* 129c–e (for an earlier echo of this dialogue see 1, 2–4 and Commentary). In Aristotle, *Eudemian Ethics* VII.9, 1241b17–24, the analogy is developed (and the master-slave comparison is added), but Aristotle distinguishes there between the natural tool (*organon sumphuton*) that body is for soul and the detachable, inanimate tool of the craftsman. In *De Anima* I.3, 407b20–26 Aristotle argues that the relation between body and soul is not a contingent one between pre-existing elements, "as if it were possible . . . for just any soul to be clothed in just any body." The craftsman-tool analogy is further developed by Aristotle here: different crafts use appropriate tools to create distinct objects, and the soul's use of the body is likewise peculiar to it, and perhaps more like the exercise of a craft than the use of a tool. In *De Anima* II.4, 415b15–20 Aristotle further refines this argument: ". . . all ensouled bodies are instruments (*organa*) of the soul . . . since they are for the sake of the soul." That is to say, the body is "an instrument used to bring the soul's activities to fruition" (Shields 2016, 204); soul is a final no less than a formal cause of a living body. Plotinus' use of the analogy here is limited to arguing that soul need not suffer affections, just as craftsmen do not suffer what their tools undergo. But we shall see that these and other details of Aristotle's refined concept of the soul-body relation influence the argument of the treatise as it develops.

3, 6–11 *But perhaps it might . . . the care of its tool*: Plotinus now suggests that the soul might be affected by sense-perception, the instrumental means by which it knows whatever external things affect it. Sight is used as an example: to see (= perception/user) is to use the eyes (= instrument). Plotinus may be influenced here by the example of the use of eyes and hands given in *Alcibiades* 129d. Sight, Plotinus argues, is not immune to harm, injury or pain any more than other bodily organs: the instrumentalist argument seems to strengthen the suggestion that the soul is somehow affected by our powers of perception. And, Plotinus adds, desires occur when soul seeks to treat or cure its body/instrument. The "treatment" or "care" (*therapeia*) of body referred to here reflects Plotinus' view that the soul which has descended from the intelligible world, and separated itself from it to become the soul of an individual body, "has left the whole and directs the individual (*to kathekaston*) with great difficulty; it is by now applying itself to and caring for (*therapeuousa*) things outside . . . and sinks deep into the individual" (IV.8.4, 18–21, trans. Armstrong, modified). But even when soul is not ensnared by body, its detachment is not devoid of care: it is, says Plotinus, elaborating the image of the soul in a plant, "as if some farmer were to become concerned about the maggots in the plant and were afflicted with worries in respect of the plant" (IV.3.4, 31–33, trans. Dillon and Blumenthal 2015). Or it is like saying that an ill person "attending to cures (*therapeiais*) for his body was concerned with the body and had come to belong to his body" (IV.3.4, 36–37, trans. Dillon and Blumenthal 2015). The radical view of Plato, *Phaedo* 66b–c (modified in later dialogues like the *Phaedrus* and *Timaeus*), that the body contaminates the soul by distracting it, and through illness and desires and other affections ("enslaved as we are to care [*therapeia(i)*] for it [sc. body]," *Phaedo* 66d1–2), influences Plotinus here (Aubry 143n14).

Plotinus explores this issue more systematically in the earlier III.6 [26]. He talks there of an affective faculty of soul (*to pathētikon*), but argues that although it is the cause of affection (III.6.4, 43–44), the soul remains unaltered and unaffected "in substrate and in substance" (III.6.3, 32). The changes and intense perceptions that we experience do happen because of the soul and have their starting points in the soul; whatever movements occur arise from the soul, but the soul is not thereby altered in substance (III.6.3, 3–26). Plotinus admits a "movement" in the soul, a natural passage from potentiality to actuality, but argues that this does not entail substantial change either (III.6.2, 44–49). He adduces the analogy with sight as the actualization of a potential (III.6.2, 34–37). Note the strong Aristotelian flavor of the argument here, particularly its use of the potentiality-actuality correlates (On III.6 see Fleet 1995). Some of these points will inform Plotinus' argument later in our treatise: on the soul's movement see 13, 3–5 with Commentary.

3, 11–17 *But how will the affections . . . separates them*: The preceding passage has identified desires that arise in the soul. In III.6.4, 1–13, Plotinus distinguishes between affections that are the result of opinions (*doxai*), such as fear of imminent death, or pleasure at the prospect of something good happening to one, and affections that occur involuntarily (*aproairetōs*), as a result of external stimuli (see Fleet 1995, 120–122). The former kind of affection, arising in the soul, is what the preceding passage in our treatise refers to. But it is the latter kinds of affection that Plotinus is referring to in the present passage, and he pinpoints the problem that they cause. If they originate in bodily events, how can they be transmitted to soul, as they must be, if they are to be consciously perceived? How can something with one nature, a substance of a particular kind, communicate with something, a nature, a substance, of a different kind?

This is the core problem of perception for Plotinus, and he will provide a solution only in Chapter 7 of the treatise. At present he is raising difficulties, asking questions. The instrumentalist model of the soul-body relation entails a user-used separation. Plotinus here reflects his Platonist concept of an immaterial soul that can exist independently of body: the terminology of separation (*chōris, chōrizei*) used here is Platonic (*Phaedo* 67c5–d10). But Aristotle also deals with the notion of separation, in the *De Anima* and elsewhere, partly as a consequence of Plato's views, partly to elucidate the concept itself. Aristotle distinguishes between spatial separation, separation by definition, and unqualified separation (e.g., *De Anima* II.2, 413b14–15; III.4, 429a10–13; III.5, 430a10–25; see Shields 2016, 80–81), and these distinctions—different uses of the term "separate" (*chōriston*)—are important for Plotinus. In the current passage he is clearly referring to unqualified, ontological separation.

3, 17–21 *But before the separation by philosophy . . . another in another way*: Plotinus now turns to another kind of separation, philosophical, of the kind advocated by Plato, *Phaedo* 67d8–10 ("and the occupation of philosophers is just this, isn't it—a release and separation of soul from body?" trans. Gallop, modified). This is at once intellectual and ethical "separation," here and now, in our bodily existence. In III.6.5, 1–2 Plotinus asks why one should strive to liberate the soul from affections "through philosophy," if it is in itself free from them. Separating soul from the body in this sense is purification, "if it (soul) turns upwards in the opposite direction from the world below" (III.6.5, 19, trans. Fleet). The influence of *Phaedo* 67c is obvious. This separation is liberation from what is lower than the best in us, freedom from subjection to the body and related wrong opinions. In the present passage Plotinus is less concerned with spelling out the nature and implications of philosophical separation than with relating it to the body-soul problem. Hence his question, "how was it?" before this separation. The subject "it" here is soul, and soul is the subject of the reply to the question: literally, "it had been mixed," that is, with body. The pluperfect tense ("had been") here is a consequence of the past tense ("was") of the preceding question: "being mixed" is prior to separation through philosophy (*ē*, line 18, replying to a question, as in 2, 19, and meaning "surely" or "the fact is"—SP, col. 473, 16–24—rather than used disjunctively, as Aubry 81n24 suggests).

Plotinus will go on to make it clear in lines 21–26 in what senses "being mixed" applies, before and after philosophical separation. But first he considers five ways in which soul could be said to be mixed with body. Option 1 is Stoic *krasis* (*di' holou*), a complete blending, which, for the Stoics, is a blend of material soul with material body. Option 2 cites Plato, *Timaeus* 36e, where the world soul is said to be "everywhere woven through (*diaplakeisa*) from the center to the outermost heaven and enveloping the heaven all round on the outside" (trans. Cornford, modified). Option 3 is Aristotle's concept of soul as the inseparable actuality of body, which does not preclude some part of soul being separable, if it is not the actuality of a body, for example, intellect or reason, *nous* (*De Anima* III.4–6). Option 4 returns to the instrumentalism of lines 3–5 of the present chapter, substituting laconically a helmsman analogy for the earlier craftsman one. The analogy echoes the no less laconic phrase of Aristotle, *De Anima* II.1, 413a8–9: "It is still unclear, however, whether the soul is the actuality of the body in the way that a sailor is of a ship" (trans. Shields: see Shields 2016, 179–181 for a discussion of the textual and philosophical problems of the passage). Aristotle's unique use of this analogy is the starting point of the development of the helmsman-ship analogy by Alexander of Aphrodisias, to which Plotinus is indebted. Alexander, *On the Soul* 14, 4–5 refers to the helmsman analogy as one of the ways in which soul might be said to be in body, only to exclude a literal interpretation of the analogy that would make the body a place where the soul is, 14, 17–19. Alexander returns at greater length to the analogy, *On the Soul* 15, 9–29, saying that if one takes the analogy to refer to the skill (*technē*) of piloting, it would illustrate how soul is in body as an immanent state (*hexis*) and form (*eidos*), immaterial and inseparable from what it is in. This is the one version of the analogy that he finds acceptable (because a thing's form makes it what it is, 15, 25–29), having rejected the basic helmsman-soul analogy (arguing *inter alia* that it makes the soul a body; that soul would be in one part of the body only; that it can enter and leave the body at will, so that the body is at one time ensouled, at another not; that its substance and nature are not thereby elucidated). *On the Soul* 20, 26–21, 21 returns to the theme, repeating some of the objections, but suggesting that the helmsman might be "the form of the ship's activity" (*tēs energeais tēs neōs eidos*) in the way that soul is the form of the living being. But even here there are difficulties, for the ship continues to exist if the helmsman leaves it, but the living being no longer lives if the soul departs (and, Alexander adds, in any case the shape or configuration of the ship, making it what it is, is a more plausible analogy for the soul).

Plotinus' extended discussion of the analogy in IV.3.21 makes some of the same points. The analogy does not account for the manner of the soul's presence in body, for the helmsman is present incidentally, and not in the whole ship. Plotinus considers the comparison with the helmsman's skill, the interpretation favored by Alexander, suggesting that it would be a skill that is immanent in the tool (here the helm). But Plotinus is not convinced, arguing that the skill originates outside the helm *qua* tool: how could one say that the skill is in the helm in the way that soul is in body (IV.3.21, 11–19)? The principal reason why Plotinus shies away from this analogy is because he cannot accept Aristotle's and Alexander's view of soul as the inseparable actuality of a living body (see Dillon and Blumenthal 2015, 268–270). The focus on the craft or skill of helmsmanship in Alexander and Plotinus is inspired by Aristotle's cryptic sentence at *De Anima* I.3, 407b25–26: "it is necessary that the craft make use of its tools, and that the soul make use of its body" (trans. Shields). Behind these uses of the analogy lies Plato's simile in which the rulers of cities are compared to true and worthless captains of ships (*Republic* VI, 488a–e).

Option 5 combines Options 3 and 4. There are no expressed nouns for "the one" and "the other": "form (*eidos*)" in Options 3 and 4 is the obvious antecedent, but the following sentence shows that Plotinus is in effect talking about "parts," that is, faculties or powers of soul. Elsewhere, if sparingly, he will employ Platonic language about parts of soul (III.6.2, 8–9, IV.8.8, 8), even if an immaterial soul is strictly speaking not divisible (language about parts is "corrected" to stress that the soul is a continuum: V.2.2, 26–29). Many instances of the use of "parts" in translations of Plotinus are translations of the *to* + adjectival noun or verbal noun form, with no Greek term corresponding to "part." It is important to realize that this is also the case here: all instances of "part" in my translation of the present passage are additions (I have used "part" because I believe the present passage alludes to the Aristotle text in *De Anima* referred to in the next paragraph, where the word *merē*, "parts," does occur). It is often less confusing to use the neutral term "faculty" (on faculties and powers of soul see Blumenthal 1971, 20–44).

Option 5 proposes that soul "parts" can relate to body in two distinct ways: the detail follows in the next sentence.

But Aristotle's influence on this distinction should first be noted, and it is the influence of the same passage in *De Anima* that contains the unique reference to the sailor-ship analogy. There, II.1, 413a6–7, having just concluded that it is "not unclear" that soul, or some parts of it, if it has natural parts, cannot be separable from body, Aristotle adds, "Even so, nothing hinders some parts from being separable, because of their not being the actualities of a body" (trans. Shields). This distinction will, *mutatis mutandis,* when the details have been filled in, become Plotinus' solution to the paradox of a soul that is at once separate and yet somehow embodied.

3, 21–26 *I mean, in so far as one part . . . or use it at all*: The final sentence of the chapter ("in so far as" translates *hē(i),* Sleeman's emendation of the manuscripts' *ē*) continues to consider Option 5, from the standpoint of "the separation by philosophy" (lines 17–18: "philosophy" here, line 24). The "using part" of soul, though separate, is nonetheless involved with body *qua* tool or instrument. Philosophy should turn or "convert" this part or faculty, as well as the faculty that is mixed with body (which is how Plotinus glosses Option 3 here, Aristotle's "unseparated form"), away from its involvement with body, except where it is necessarily involved (presumably in making the body a living, functional body. Marzolo 2006, 112 plausibly suggests that the phrase "in so far as there is not absolute necessity," line 25, cites the thematically close passage in *Phaedo* 67a2–4, where it is said that we get closest to knowledge when we keep ourselves as detached from the body as we can, "except where there is absolute necessity" that we commune with it. The phrase echoes that of V.1.12, 18–19, and the theme is similar, the "separation" from undue involvement with the body through philosophy. In the present passage Plotinus distinguishes between temporary separation (such as a specific intellection of a Form) and complete intellectual withdrawal (when soul fully activates its union with Intellect). At V.1.10, 24–31 he explains what such separation entails, suggesting there, as in the present passage, that the lower soul power may also be led toward purification, whether "led above" or "led away." Tornau 427n12 draws attention to the relevance of these two passages in V.1 to the present text. On "amphibious" souls living "in turn the life There, and the life here," and in different proportions, see IV.8.4, 31–35.

Plotinus, then, is referring to the "conversion" (*epistrophē*) of the soul, extricating it from temporal concerns, but he is referring to this cardinal theme of his philosophy in a truncated way, focusing on "conversion from" the body, rather than on the implicit "conversion to" soul's higher intellectual life. This is in keeping with the schematic and speculative tone of the chapter and of this stage of the treatise's argument. But Option 5, as here presented, adumbrates Plotinus' solution in the treatise's later chapters to the problems and questions raised at this stage.

In line 26 *mē . . . mēde* is usually understood to be an emphatic negative ("not even"): the final phrase of the chapter could then be translated: "so that it does not even use it all the time." The phrase is odd, and Theiler, following Volkmann, deleted *mēde* (HBT Vb, 441). But this is not necessary. One can, with Tornau 314, understand *mē* . . . *mēde* disjunctively, "(a) not . . . (b) not at all" (for the latter see LSJ, *mēde* B), with a shared verb "use."

Chapter 4

Plotinus continues to consider the concept of a soul-body "mixture," reviewing, in varying detail, the five options of the previous chapter. His argument moves from rhetorical exaggeration to lapidary assertion, with shorthand but significant allusions to Aristotelian analysis. The key issues of perception and the affections resurface, as does the notion of the soul's impassivity. There is some progress in formulating a tenable account of the relation between soul and body, and the chapter concludes by positing the "living thing," introduced in the previous chapter, as the subject of the affections.

4, 1–10 *Let us assume then . . . and it will be subject to destruction*: In the previous chapter, Plotinus has used the verb "to be mixed" to refer to a number of different soul-body relations. He begins this chapter with the same verb, but seems immediately to confine it to something like Stoic "(through-and-through) blending" (*krasis (di' holou)*, see 3, 19). But he does not engage seriously with the Stoic concept here. He had treated it in an earlier essay, II.7, arguing against it on the grounds that there cannot be complete transfusion of independently existing bodies (and thereby misunderstanding the Stoics, under the influence of the Peripatetic critique of Alexander of Aphrodisias). Here he applies a very un-Stoic dualistic model to the concept, contrasting a superior, living, rational soul with a lifeless body. Given this model, mixture can only be better for body (it imports life into it) and worse for soul, which is infected by the body's lifelessness and unreason. He argues that the soul, its life truncated, cannot be supposed to acquire perception. Perception, following this model, will be a function of the living body, as will its attendant affections, such as desire and fear. Aubry 155–159 is undoubtedly right to identify the rhetorical tone of this passage. It does less justice to the Stoic concept than Plotinus' more nuanced discussion of it in IV.7.8[2] (on which see Fleet 2016, 179–188). It introduces a concept of soul that is closer to Plato's (in, for instance, *Phaedo* 66b–d) than to the Stoic "breath" principle (*pneuma*). But at the same time, it suggests a counter-model (Aubry 157–158), glimpsed in the preceding chapters through references to the soul's immateriality and impassivity. In IV.7.8[2], 20–22 Plotinus, rejecting the Stoic concept of blending, wants to save the "through-and-through" aspect of soul-body mixture, but suggests that this is only possible if soul is immaterial. Later in the same treatise, in an argument that is reminiscent of the present passage, he argues that soul *qua* primary and eternal being cannot be a dead thing (like a stone), but, even if it is mixed with "what is worse" and impeded in its relation to "what is best," its nature cannot be destroyed (IV.7.9, 26–29). These are elements of the argument of the later chapters of our treatise. But, in addition to suggesting the counter-model, the present passage highlights the essential role of body in perception and the affections, even if it is not yet quite clear how body and soul function in such processes.

4, 10–12 *Also, the mode of this mixture . . . a line is mixed with white*: This sentence is an appendix to the preceding argument. The blending hypothesis raises the question of what kinds of mixture are possible. The example of "a line mixed with white" derives from Aristotle, *On Generation and Corruption* I 7, 323b23–27, where different views on action and being affected are discussed. Aristotle argues that "if . . . two things are absolutely other, that is, in no respect identical," they cannot affect each other: "Whiteness could not be affected in any way by a line nor a line by whiteness—except perhaps accidentally, namely if the line happened to be white or black" (trans. Joachim in Barnes 1984, 529, modified). Given the presuppositions about soul and body in the preceding argument, where it is evident that he posits their absolute difference, Plotinus finds Aristotle's view attractive. He also refers to the example of the colored line in III.6.9, 12–13, as one instance of things being present to one another with no accompanying alteration or affection. His brief mention of the example here makes the same point by implication: the mixture of two intrinsically different kinds of thing does not necessarily entail that one is affected by the other. For Plotinus' extended use of *On Generation and Corruption* I 7 in III.6.9 see Fleet 1995, 188–192.

4, 12–18 *And the "being woven through" . . . it will suffer the body's affections*: Plotinus turns to Option 2 of the preceding chapter (see Commentary 3, 17–21), citing again the key term "woven through" from *Timaeus* 36e. His concern here, apart from giving the impression of doing justice to Plato's view, is to use this option as an argument for the soul's impassivity, and he does this by the briefest of allusions to the example of light. The light analogy is developed in IV.3.22, part of a long section (Chapters 19–23) in that treatise exploring the soul's embodiment. There Plotinus gives the example of fire (focusing on its provision of light) which, "while being present, is not present" (for the phrase see also the present treatise, 11, 11, and Commentary 11, 8–13), permeating the air without being mixed with any part of it, for "it stays where it is while the air flows by" (IV.3.22, 1–4, trans. Dillon and Blumenthal). This light analogy will be retained by Plotinus as an apt way of illustrating the soul's presence to body. As with the next two options discussed, Plotinus finds elements of an acceptable account of the body-soul relation in Option 2 (on IV.3.22 see Dillon and Blumenthal 2015, 270–271; Blumenthal 1971, 18–19).

4, 18–27 *But will it be in the body like form . . . rather the living thing does so*: Plotinus considers Options 3 and 4 together (and so *de facto* Option 5 also), as both posit soul's presence in body as form (*eidos*), whether the latter is separable or inseparable. Plotinus argues that the first alternative is favourable to the instrumentalist interpretation (it also happens to be Plato's view, though that is not stated explicitly here), but he devotes more space to the second Aristotelian alternative, which will prove fruitful in accounting for soul-body interaction. The comparison of soul-body with an axe derives from Aristotle, *De Anima* II 1, 412b11–15. If, Aristotle argues, one were to consider a tool like an axe to be a natural body, its substance, or soul, would be what it is to be an axe, its essence, that is, as a cutting instrument (its actuality is cutting, 412b27–28). If it loses this function, it is no longer an axe. Plotinus takes from this comparison the assumption behind it, that an axe is iron shaped in a particular way, and posits that the resultant "combination," the *sunamphoteron* (line 21: one of a number of terms used by Plotinus to refer to soul-body: see Commentary 5, 1–2), namely the shape (*schēma*, here = form) and the iron, constitute the axe. The axe is iron shaped in a specific way to perform a function (in Aristotelian terms, to actualize its potentiality as a cutting instrument), to do what an axe does, in accordance with its shape (or form). Without the Aristotelian comparison, Plotinus' adaptation of Aristotle would make less sense, but it is nonetheless a creative adaptation. Plotinus could not, for instance, concur with Aristotle's comment in the same chapter of *De Anima*, that it is "unnecessary to ask whether soul and body are one" (412b6).

Plotinus is interested in the axe comparison because he believes that it throws light on the location of the affections (the opening question of the treatise). He infers that the axe's shape, the "soul" of the axe in his reading of the comparison, enables the axe to perform specific functions. Likewise, he argues, the body, shaped or formed as it is by soul (that is the sense of "a particular sort of body" in line 24, part of the citation of Aristotle discussed below), can experience the affections common (*koina*) to it and soul. He has still to explain how this happens and what the roles of soul and body are: he will begin to give his explanation in the next chapters. Committed as he is to an impassive soul, he must consider the issues of affections and perception in relation to each element of the "combination" of body and soul. He cannot subscribe to Aristotle's hylomorphism, but that does not prevent him from citing most of Aristotle's definition (or definitions: see Ackrill 1997) of soul in *De Anima* II.1. There soul is said to be "the first actuality of a natural (*phusikou*) body which has life in potentiality (*dunamei zōēn ekhontos*)," adding "this sort of (*toiouton*) body would be one which is organic (*organikon*)" (412a27–b1, trans. Shields). Plotinus quotes the terms underlined, but omits the reference to "actuality," which is the key to Aristotle's understanding of hylomorphism. The term *organikon*, translated "organic" in both Aristotle and Plotinus here, most likely refers to the body as an organ of the soul, but it can also mean "fitted with organs," as well as alluding to the instrumentalist thesis (see Shields 2016, 171–173). The fact that he gives the definition as one of body rather than soul is in the spirit of Aristotle's argument. It suits him to stay this close to Aristotle here, for he wants us to focus on the "living thing" (*zō(i)on*) in line 27, the body-soul entity introduced at the start of Chapter 3 (see Commentary 3, 1–3), which becomes central to his analysis from the next chapter on.

Aristotle is cited once more in this chapter (line 26), from his critique of earlier arguments that the soul is in self-motion when we experience affections: "saying that the soul is angry would be like saying that the soul weaves or builds. For it is perhaps better not to say that the soul pities or learns or thinks, but that the human being does these things with the soul" (*De Anima* I.4, 408b11–15, trans. Shields). Plotinus can subscribe to this, and Aristotle's references to "human being" as agent and to the soul as instrument will influence him in later chapters of the treatise (see 5, 29–34; 13, 1–2).

Chapter 5

The chapter begins by considering various ways of understanding "living thing" as applied to humans, eventually focusing on it as the "common entity" or "combination" of soul-body. Plotinus' concern now is to account for affections and impulses (distress, pain, desire, sexual appetite) in which both a faculty or power of soul and a bodily state or disposition appear to be involved. Belief and judgment are taken into consideration as parts of the process, and certain appetites, such as desire for the Good, are asserted to be the soul's alone, just as certain beliefs (e.g., about the presence of a threat) need not entail an accompanying affection. Once again, Plotinus enumerates the difficulties without providing solutions, though the increasingly specific nature of the problems prepares the way for his solutions. Toward the end of the chapter he introduces the "human being" as the subject of appetites, alongside the specific soul-faculty. This anticipates his concept of the "we" or self, which comes into play from Chapter 7 on.

5, 1–2 *But one should say . . . come into being from both*: Plotinus, focusing on the "living thing" (*zō(i)on*) of Chapters 3–4, provides three optional ways of describing it. The trio of options is reminiscent of 1, 2–4, but only superficially. Now Plotinus is concentrating on the third option of that opening passage, and analysing it. For the living thing is compacted of body and soul (3, 2–3). Is it (1) the "body of such a kind," the "so-qualified body"? This term (*toionde sōma*) is Aristotle's (*De Anima* II.1, 412a16–17), in a context where he is arguing that the soul cannot be identified with a living body. Plotinus will not explore this option further here (lines 7–8), and when he returns to the term in Chapter 7 he uses it to describe the complex material substrate, formed by the world soul, into which the soul that forms the living being enters (see Commentary 7, 1–6). Is the living thing (2) the "common entity" (*to koinon*; see 4, 24), that is, body-soul? The term is again Aristotle's (*De Anima* I.4, 408b28–29). It is generally equivalent to the "combination" (*sunamphoteron*) of 4, 21 and 5, 8 (this latter term refers to the body-soul combination in Plato, *Symposium* 209b7 and *Timaeus* 87e5–6, and in *Alcibiades* 130a9). Option (2) is Plotinus' favourite, though the relation of soul to body has to be explained. The inclusion of a further option (3) here is therefore largely for formal completeness. This option must refer to a fusion of the two elements, body and soul, in a third distinct entity. Such fusion was explicitly distinguished by Stoics from their concept of blending, in which the blended elements retain their properties and remain separable (LS §48C = SVF II 473). Marzolo 2006, 121 suggests that Plotinus' third option here is equivalent to the *sunamphoteron* of *Alcibiades* 130a9, but there is no suggestion of fusion there, and in any case Plotinus is now considering descriptions of the living thing, not definitions of "man," the theme of the *Alcibiades* passage.

5, 3–7 *But whatever may be the case . . . suffer in a different way*: The problem of accounting for affections remains, irrespective of how the living thing is described. Plotinus develops two alternatives here, neither at this stage of the argument satisfactory: either soul remains impassive *qua* cause "of this kind of thing," that is, affections (to be understood from the immediate context), or it must be identically or similarly affected as the living thing. Plotinus explains this latter possibility by arguing that the living thing will be affected, for example by desire, and the "desiring faculty" (the *epithumētikon*, by which he means the soul's power or capacity of desiring) will be affected by the same desire, but in a different way from the living thing. Or will it act (for it must still be the cause) rather than be affected? In a general sense, Plotinus is probably influenced here by Aristotle's discussion in *De Anima* III.10 of how the desiring faculty (the *orektikon*) is "something producing motion while being moved," whereas the *zō(i)on* is simply moved (III.10, 433b16–18). Later in this chapter Plotinus will show how, for him, *epithumētikon* and *orektikon* are related.

5, 7–8 *Now the "body of a certain sort" is to be considered later*: See 7, 1–6 with Commentary.

5, 8–16 *But the combination—how, for instance, can it be distressed . . . the soul's or the combination's*: The "combination," *sunamphoteron*, has already been referred to in 4, 21, and refers here to what Plotinus has called the *koinon*, the "common entity," in 5, 2. The body-soul conjoint has not yet been adequately described, and Plotinus continues to raise problems that a persuasive description must solve. The example of the affection of distress (*lupē*) is considered. Is the body in a distressed state, and does the affection "get through" (*dielthontos*) to the perceptive faculty, hence to soul? Plotinus may be thinking of accounts of bodily transmission to soul found in Plato's *Timaeus* 45d, 64a–c, and 67b–c to explain respectively seeing, pleasure and pain, and hearing (see Aubry 85n46). The verb used to express "transmitting" in these passages (*diadidonai*) becomes a technical term, the noun *diadosis*, in Stoic accounts of perception. Plotinus engages in polemic against the Stoic view in IV.1.2 and IV.7.7, but there it is the materialist nature of the account that he objects to. Plotinus is unlikely to be thinking of the Stoics here, but even with the support of Plato's authority he can propose no easy explanation of transmission: it is, like much else in these chapters, a puzzle (on transmission see further 6, 10–12). Perception has yet to be accounted for.

It is often assumed that lines 12–15 refer to the Stoic view that the passions (but not all affections) are based on false value-judgments or mistaken beliefs of the rational governing-faculty. In fact, belief and judgment, true and mistaken, play an important role in Plotinus' developed account of perception and affections (see 9, 1–12). Plotinus's difficulty has to do, not with the role of judgment per se in affections (introduced here, to be exploited later) but, once again, with accounting for the experience of concomitant pain in the body and the living thing. Or, as he adds here, it is unclear, in cases where pain is involved, whose is the belief, the soul's or the combination's (= living thing).

5, 17–21 *Besides, the opinion about evil . . . How then are these affections common?*: Plotinus next observes that it is possible to have opinions that some evil is present, or that one is looked down on, or that a particular appetite is for something good, without suffering distress, or anger, or arousal. These cases seem to imply that opinions are independent of affections. But in that case how (if, as he has been suggesting, opinions nonetheless play a role in affections, as do judgments,) can affections be common to soul and body? The problems persist.

In line 17 I follow (with Tornau 330) the reading of several manuscripts, adopted by HS_1, *toû kakon*, rather than Theiler's emendation *tou* (unaccented) *kakon* (HBT Vb, 443), which HS_2 adopts. In the former case, one has to supply, after *toû kakon*, the words *ti pareinai*, expressed in line 13 but not here: the phrase means "Besides, the belief about evil being present . . ." This is severe ellipsis, but there is no difficulty in understanding the meaning. Theiler's emendation, in which unaccented *tou* = *tinos*, gives the sense "Besides, the belief about somebody's evil . . ." would allude to lines 13–14, the belief that evil is present to oneself or someone of one's kinsfolk.

5, 21–26 *Is it because desire belongs . . . as in the case of sex*: Plotinus' presentation here of a soul with several faculties or powers is typical of partial appropriation of Aristotle's concept of soul. Here "in general" (*holōs*) suggests that the appetitive (*orektikon*) faculty is subdivided into (at least) desiring and irascible faculties. The metaphor of "stretching/reaching out" in *orexis* and related verb forms is mirrored here in the use of "stretching out" (*ektasis*, the reading of one MS, adopted by HS_2 and most modern commentators and translators; most MSS have *extasis*, "movement out") in line 23. On the importance of the appetitive faculty (*orektikon*) in Aristotle's psychology see his *De Anima* III.10.

No sooner has Plotinus identified soul powers, and momentarily suggested that they are not common to soul and body, than he immediately corrects himself: when appetite is aroused, the body is in a certain state, and blood and bile boil. There is a reminiscence here of what Aristotle says about anger as a boiling of blood and heat around the heart, according to the natural scientist (*De Anima* I.1, 403a29–b1), who would define anger differently from the philosopher.

Indeed, Plotinus is probably thinking of the whole section (I.1, 403a16–b19) on ways in which affections of the soul involve the body. The reference to sex here may be anticipated in Chapter 2, 19 (see Commentary 2, 13–25). Plotinus is still identifying problems, asking questions: at present, to put it crudely, he seems to be developing a parallelism between soul powers and bodily affections, but the connection between them is not yet clear, although he is suggesting, with ever greater emphasis, that it is necessary.

5, 26–28 *And it should be granted . . . to the common entity*: There are, however, certain appetites or desires that are the soul's alone, such as desire for the Good. The definite article here (*tou agathou)*, and the assertion that body is not involved, means that, out of the blue, Plotinus points toward the activity of the intellectual power of soul, and its striving after the first principle of everything, the Good or One. Plotinus returns in Chapter 8 to our intellect (*nous*) and its relation to Intellect. The *tis* in *tis logos*, line 28, is difficult to translate. The most obvious versions (see Marzolo 2006, 125), taking this as generalizing or as referring to a specific teaching, give a meaning that is either unsatisfactorily vague or over-precise. Plotinus may simply mean no more than "upon reflection" (so Tornau 316), as he states what, for him, is obvious, even if he has not integrated it, at least in this treatise, into his account of affections.

5, 29–35 *But when a man longs for sex . . . where will it start from?*: Plotinus returns to sexual appetite: the appetitive power of soul will desire, but so will "the man." Why the introduction of a new term, "man" (*sensu stricto* "human being," *anthrōpos*), here? Apart from being the second part of the title of the treatise, it provides a reminder of the *Alcibiades*, where a definition of "man" is sought. But more importantly, it moves beyond the problematic "common entity," and the attempt to provide answers by concentrating on soul-body unity-in-duality. Tornau 428 is probably right to suggest that Plotinus is here pointing toward the introduction of a concept of the "we" or self in Chapter 7 as a solution to his difficulties. But for the time being, despite the terminological shift, the problems remain: where does appetite originate, in the man or in the appetitive faculty? Plotinus ends the chapter with a reiteration of the hen-egg dilemma, here in the case of the affections (do they depend on a bodily predisposition?); but it is of course also a problem in accounting for perception.

Chapter 6

Plotinus posits a new hypothesis in this chapter. He examines the consequences of the assumption (contradicting what he has been arguing in the previous chapter) that the various affective faculties (which he here, as often, calls "powers") are not in themselves affected, but somehow transmit their powers to the "combination." This assumption may save the soul's impassivity, but it creates insurmountable problems in accounting for affections and perception. It seems to imply a perceptive soul-power that does not perceive, or even a soul that lacks the life that the "combination" has. And if these impossible implications were correct, then even the combination's capacity to perceive or be affected would be questionable. Plotinus has created an argumentative impasse, but has also prepared the ground for the solution to his dilemmas, and this solution will follow in the next chapters.

6, 1–7 *But perhaps it is better . . . belong to what has them*: Plotinus starts tentatively ("perhaps it is better to say") with a new sequence of hypothetical suggestions. "Powers" (*dunameis*) is the term commonly used by him to refer to the various faculties of soul. It should be remembered that the term "faculty" used in the preceding chapters is a translation of *to* + adjectival/verbal noun phrases, where a word corresponding to "faculty" or "part" does not occur (see Commentary 3, 17–21). "Power" recurs with the same reference later in the present chapter in the phrases "power of perception" (9) and "soul-power" (16). There is no ambiguity in its use here, despite the general application of Aristotelian vocabulary in the treatise: these powers are unmoved (3), like soul itself, and so in no sense potentialities, though they provide the capacity to act (*to dunasthai*, 3) to whatever has them (Aubry 183–186). Though Plotinus is initially vague about what has these powers, it becomes clear that he means the living thing or "combination" (4–5).

In asserting that the powers are unmoved, Plotinus abandons the assumption of the previous chapter that the affective faculties are, or must be, themselves moved when one desires, etc. We are on new ground here. Striking conclusions follow. Firstly, soul ("the cause of life") may remain impassive, while the living thing acts or suffers. This conclusion, suitably refined, will become part of Plotinus' solution.

My translation of lines 4–7 follows Theiler's interpretation (HBT Vb, 444), adopted by HS_2, that is, *esti* (4) means "it is possible," followed by an accusative and infinitive construction ("that . . . the cause of life . . . is impassive"), and *autēn* (5) is reflexive ("itself"). It remains to be explained in what way soul "gives itself" to the living thing, while remaining impassive (see 7, 1–6).

6, 7–10 *But if this is so . . . that which has the power*: The next conclusions are shocking, and Tornau 428 is surely right to find them presented as impossibilities: (a) life (after all, an essential characteristic of soul) will not belong to soul, but to the combination; (b) the power of perception does not perceive. Plotinus seems to have gained precious little from the new hypothesis of the preceding lines. But we shall see that his argument is of tactical importance. Plotinus seems immediately to qualify conclusion (a) by saying that the combination's life would not be soul's life (8–9), that is, that we would have to define "life" differently in each case; but this does not let him off the hook, as lines 14–16 (see Commentary 6, 10–16) demonstrate.

In lines 7–8 note the sense of *kai* ("also," i.e., in addition to affections and activities belonging, not to soul but to the combination, soul will lack life) and of *holōs ou* ("not at all," see SP, col. 735, 15–19).

6, 10–16 *But if perception is a movement . . . if neither soul nor the soul-power are included in it?*:

Plotinus repeats the view of 5, 9–11, adding that it seems to entail that soul perceives. But he wants to maintain conclusion (b) for the time being, and so speculates that if the capacity to perceive is present in the combination, it, that is, the combination, will self-consciously perceive (*ē*, 12, "well," assertively introduces the proposed answer to the question how the soul will not perceive).

My translation of lines 12–14 follows HS_2, adopted by most modern versions. It depends on E. R. Dodds's emendation of interrogative *tí* in lines 14. Dodds proposed the insertion of *ho* before a non-interrogative, unaccented *ti*: ". . . what it perceives." Aubry 88 retains the manuscripts' text (following HS_1), which gives the sense ". . . through its (i.e., the power of perception's) presence it will perceive. What will perceive? The combination." HS_1 inserted a question mark after "the combination," which makes the manuscripts' text a bit less plodding, but Dodds's neat emendation preserves the hypothetical tone more fluently. Either way, the problem formulated in the chapter's final sentence remains. Granted an unmoved soul-power, and granted that neither soul nor the soul-power are in the combination, how can the combination perceive?

Chapter 7

This chapter is the turning point of the treatise. Having discussed problems and difficulties in most of the preceding chapters, Plotinus now begins to offer solutions, some of the implications of which will only become apparent as the treatise proceeds. He introduces the concept of the soul-trace, using a light metaphor here, to account for the presence of soul in the combination. This will help to elucidate the bodily element in perception; it will also allow Plotinus to argue that something can be ensouled and subject to affections, without the soul itself being affected. The chapter also gives a condensed account of how perception functions. It provides the first of a number of allusions to Plato's texts in the later chapters of the treatise: these allusions, by citation and exegesis, link the treatise's argument to the authority of Plato. Finally, it introduces the key concept of the "we" or self and the related concept of what is "ours," and briefly explores the "we" at the level of the reasoning or intellectual soul.

7, 1–6 *Right! Suppose . . . affections of the living thing*: The chapter opens with a resounding *ē*, almost colloquially, hence the translation "Right!" The affirmation that follows inaugurates the second part of the treatise, in which solutions and answers will be provided. The opening sentence replies to the question concluding the previous chapter, asserting strongly that it is the combination that perceives (see Marzolo 2006, 128–129). Plotinus begins with a compact statement of his view that soul does not descend into body (see IV.8.8, 1–6; on the theme in general, see Blumenthal 1971, 15–19). Here he describes what does enter body as "some kind of light (*phōs*)." Elsewhere he speaks of an image (*eidōlon*, see IV.3.10, 38–40; see also 11, 11–13 below, on soul in animals), a trace (*ichnos*, see IV.4.28, 52–55 and 29, 50–51; VI.4.15, 8–18), an appearance (*indalma*, see V.9.6, 15–20), a shadow (*skia*, see IV.4.18, 6–7) or an irradiation (*ellampsis*, see VI.4.3, 19–23, where the verbal form occurs; for the noun see Chapter 11, 14 below, on soul in animals). The soul does not give itself "constituted as it is" (i.e., being intellectual and impassive) either to the combination or to the "other component," that is, the body. The body is also described as "constituted as it is," that is, already animated by the lower soul powers and so disposed as to receive the soul-trace. This qualification of body is reminiscent of Aristotle's argument that there must be some commonality between soul and body (*De Anima* I.3, 407b13–26). The "body such as it is" (*sōma toiouton*) here echoes "the body so-qualified" (*sōma toionde*) or "of such-and-such-a-kind" (natural, potentially having life, with organs) of *De Anima* II.1, 412a16–21. The latter term (already used in 5, 1 and 8: see Commentary 5, 1–2) occurs in IV.4.20–21, in a discussion, anticipating the present treatise, of the question of the subject of desires: he concludes that it is the "the body so-qualified." Plotinus expresses the idea of commonality by saying that body receives soul in accordance with its "aptitude" (*epitēdeiotēs*), VI.4.15, 1–8. Plotinus' choice of this term is most likely influenced by its occurrence in Alcinous and Alexander of Aphrodisias (Tornau 1998, 219–220; Emilsson and Strange 2015, 26–28, 150–151, 201–202; Lee 1979; O'Meara 1980). For Plotinus the body "so-qualified" has its vegetative and nutritive powers (see IV.9.3, 23–8) directly from the world-soul (see Blumenthal 1971, 27–30), and in a more general sense world-soul is said to prepare "dwellings" for individual souls and "draw a preliminary outline" which individual souls complete (see IV.3.6, 10–15; VI.7.7, 8–17). The theme of the soul-trace is treated by Plotinus in IV.3.19–23 and especially in IV.4.18–21 and 28–29 (on these texts see Dillon and Blumenthal 2015, 256–276, 373–386, 409–417; Noble 2013 focuses on IV.4.18). Caluori 2015, 186–192 elucidates the distinction between the soul-trace and the powers and activities of the qualified body. The present passage and the concept of the soul-trace are analyzed by Emilsson 2017, 230–235.

Plotinus may be using "nature" (*phusis*, 5) here, as often in Aristotle, to refer to the "essence" of the living thing. When he calls the latter "something distinct," he means something distinct from soul, not something in which soul and a body are transmuted into a new entity. This living thing will be the subject of perceptions and other affections. Having asserted this, Plotinus must now give the assertion substance. He begins to do so in the following lines by giving an account of perception.

7, 6–16 *But how do we perceive? . . . opinions and intellections come*: Plotinus has been suggesting that it is the living thing, the combination, that perceives (6, 12–14; 7, 3–6), but also that the soul may perceive (6, 10–12). Here he shifts the focus to the "we" (*hēmeis*). The inclusion of the pronoun in line 6 gives it emphasis: how is it that we perceive? He suggests immediately the range of the "we": our whole human substance embraces the living thing and other, higher, at present unspecified, elements. He then proceeds to give a highly condensed account of perception, the brevity of which creates difficulties. The difficulties are also partly due to the wide range of meanings of "to perceive" (*aisthanesthai*) that Plotinus inherits from the philosophical tradition; *aisthanesthai, aisthēsis*, and related terms can refer to sensation, to sense-perception, as well as to mental or intellectual perception (see Commentary 1, 11–13). Deciding its reference in its various uses in this chapter is crucial. In lines 9–12 Plotinus talks of the soul's perception being perception, not of *aisthēta*, but of *noēta*. The *aisthēta-noēta* contrast must refer to sense-objects as opposed to mental "objects" or intelligibles.

Blumenthal's analysis of this passage suggests that Plotinus is claiming here that sense-perception is not perception of external objects, but of something cognized (Blumenthal 1971, 72; 1976, 47). This appears to imply a representational or antirealist view of perception that would run counter to Plotinus' repeated assertions that we perceive the external world itself (IV.4.23, 15–19; IV.5.1, 1–13; IV.6.1, 14–40; for these and further references see Emilsson 1988, 8 with n18). Emilsson has, surely correctly, argued that the soul's perception in lines 9–12 cannot refer to sense-perception, if it is perception of "intelligibles" (*noēta*). Plotinus has, in this briefest of accounts, begun at the end of the process of accounting for perception. He is referring here to a kind of apprehension by the soul of internalized images—which, as often, he calls "impressions" (*tupoi*)—deriving from sensation. This apprehension, as will be seen, is the necessary cognitive aspect of perception: it is what translates sensation into perception. But it is not itself **sense**-perception. Sensation (that must be the meaning of *aisthēsis* in line 10), on the other hand, generates these "impressions" in the living thing (lines 10–11), and this "external" sensation (*aisthēsis* in line 12) is a mere "likeness" (*eidōlon*) of the soul's perception.

In lines 13–14 Plotinus contrasts sensation with the soul's perception: the latter is contemplation of "Forms alone"—the *noēta* of line 12—"alone" because free of any bodily admixture, and it is contemplation in which the soul is unaffected or impassive (an essential characteristic of

Plotinus' Platonist concept of soul). The forms contemplated are the Platonic Forms, intuited by the soul independently of embodiment: the "soul . . . alone" of line 15 refers to this state, when the soul is one with Intellect (*nous*), and from which it does not descend even when embodied. The soul's possession of the Forms makes perception possible, in that it enables the soul to identify and evaluate the data of sensation (see Blumenthal 1971, 78–79). Plotinus' reference to "reasonings and opinions" in line 16 is, at least in part, a reference to the evaluative, judging role of the soul in perception (and the beginnings of an answer to the questions of 1, 7–9). In Chapter 9 of the treatise Plotinus discusses the nature of this judging role and the problem of the fallibility of our opinions.

There are fuller accounts of sense-perception elsewhere in Plotinus, of which IV.4.23 is perhaps the most helpful and interesting (for the following see Blumenthal 1971, 76–77; Emilsson 1988, 90–93; Dillon and Blumenthal 2015, 393–396). Sensation somehow transmits in a non-conceptual way the quality of sense-objects, which soul comprehends as immaterial forms in matter. Soul cannot apprehend sense-objects on its own ("alone" here in IV.4.23, 4, and later in line 13, refers, not to soul's pre-embodied existence, but to the impossibility of soul being able on its own to grasp a sense-object). So there must be a third thing that receives the quality, the form of the sense-object, and that enables perception of such features as shape, color, and distance. This third element must be subject to affection, it must be similar to the sense-object and so able to assimilate it, while not being identical (in substance) with it. This mediating element sounds, as Dillon observes, very like the notion of the pneumatic vehicle posited by some Middle Platonists and later Neoplatonists, but which Plotinus does not adopt (Dillon 2013; Dillon and Blumenthal 2015, 394–395). In our treatise this function of the third element seems to be fulfilled by the living thing, which somehow enables the intellectual soul to apprehend the impressions that are produced in it (7, 10–11), presumably because of the presence of the image or reflection of soul present in the living thing, whose sensations are among its affections (see above on 7, 1–6).

7, 16–18 *And it is precisely there . . . over the living thing*: Although he introduced the discussion of sense-perception in line 6 with an explicit reference to the "we" or self, Plotinus' sketch of sense-perception in this chapter has not depended on the concept of the self. But he returns to it now, and asserts that it is precisely the activity of the soul's perception, and the related activities generally of discursive reasoning (the *logikē psuchē* of line 22) and judgment, where "we above all are." This empirical psychic self typically constitutes our identity in our life in the world, and it is the master element that oversees the living thing (lines 15–16, 18). But this does not mean that Plotinus intends thereby to delimit the scope of the self or "we," as will shortly be seen.

Sometimes Plotinus employs the distinction "we-ours" to distinguish between the self and what is also characteristic of our constitution or our activities. He does so here with regard to Intellect—here "the things before these"—as "ours." He explores our relation to Intellect further in the following chapter.

7, 18–24 *There will be no impediment . . . activities of the soul*: Here Plotinus does with the concept of "living thing" what he will later, in 10, 5–7, do with the concept of the "we," namely extend its scope or range. It can, as in 3, 2–3 and in *Phaedrus* 246c5 (Plotinus' source for the concept), include the lower faculties and "what comes next" (here, lines 19–20, in the sense of what is higher than these lower faculties: in lines 17–18 "what comes next" refers to what is lower than Intellect). The lower element is "mixed" in that it includes both soul-trace and body. The higher aspect of this extended description of the living thing (the reasoning soul of the preceding lines) is now called "the true man," thereby introducing an echo of Plato's *Republic* 589a7–b1 (where "the man within" occurs: on Platonic themes and exegesis in these later chapters of I.1 see Szlezák 1979, 200–202). Note that Plotinus qualifies "the true man" by *schedon*, which usually adds a tentative or softening tone: "so to speak" ("mehr oder weniger," Tornau; Armstrong's "I suppose," is perhaps a touch too tentative).

What a human being really is cannot be reduced to a formula or a single level of being, any more than the "we" can. The "true man" reappears nevertheless at 10, 7. Plotinus is not just influenced by one Platonic term here: the next sentence of the present chapter provides a condensed allusive exegesis of *Republic* IX, 588c–590b. Plato's "image of the soul" (588b10) in this passage combines the human being with a "variegated animal" (588c7) and the "lion-like" (588d3, 590a9–b1) element: the image of a human being is added as an outer covering, giving the impression that it is a single being and not the tripartite creature within. Plato is using this image to illustrate his concept of the tripartite soul, found here in the *Republic* as well as in the *Phaedrus*: the variegated animal is the appetitive part, the lion represents the spirited part, the man within the reasoning, thinking part. Although Plotinus concludes the sentence with the reasoning soul, he is more concerned to invoke Plato's general authority than the specific tripartition concept here. In fact, he is suggesting a bipartite rational-irrational distinction, in which beast and lion are aspects of one element (*holōs*, "in short," line 21, emphasizes that they are a pair). Plotinus refers to Plato's tripartition from time to time, but generally employs the bipartite distinction, or an account of a wider range of soul powers, as more satisfactory descriptions of the soul (Blumenthal 1971, 21–30; Wilberding 2006, 177 usefully lists the range of divisions of the soul found in Plotinus).

Plotinus calls the rational soul "reasoning (*logikē*) soul" and its "reasonings" *logismoi* in lines 22–23, no doubt alluding to Plato's term *logistikon* for the reasoning soul-part in the *Republic*. These reasonings are the same as the *dianoiai* of line 16. There may be a suggestion that the "we" is to be equated with whatever faculty or power of ours is consciously active (a view that Plotinus expresses elsewhere: V.1.12, 5–21) in the assertion "when we reason, it is *we* (*hēmeis* expressed and hence emphatic: see 7, 6 and Commentary 7, 6–16) who reason," lines 22–23.

Chapter 8

*This chapter continues the programme announced in Chapter 1, turning attention to Intellect and its intellections (*noēseis*) or Forms (1, 8–9). Having introduced the concept of the "we" or self in the previous chapter, Plotinus considers how we can be said to possess Intellect, and in what ways we have the Forms. The highest principle, the Good or One (here "the God"), is introduced, and the question of our relation to it, but the main focus of the chapter remains the relation between soul and body, and the nature of the presence of the soul-trace in the living being or "combination." The soul's creative role, and its range of faculties or powers in its embodied condition, are briefly explored.*

8, 1–8 *But how are we in relation to Intellect? . . . in Intellect all together*: Plotinus immediately makes it clear that his reference to Intellect (*nous*) in the opening question is to the hypostasis Intellect ("Intellect itself," lines 2–3): on it, and its identity with its objects, the "intelligibles" (*noēta*), see V.5.1 (with commentary by Gerson 2013, 57–97). He distinguishes it from the "state" (*hexis*) of the soul, deriving from transcendent Intellect ("above us," line 3): this is the rational or reasoning soul of the previous chapter, which knows the Forms. This is a permanent characteristic of the soul—which is why he calls it a "state" (*hexis*)—and so "ours"; but it has to be consciously activated, as he later explains (see 9, 14–15; 9, 18–23 with Commentary 9, 12–15; 9, 15–23). Because it is an indivisible ("without parts," *ameristos*, line 5) unity, we possess it, paradoxically, in common with all who possess it, and at the same time as fully our own: Plotinus has developed this paradox in the treatise VI.4–5. The "first soul" (line 6) which possesses Intellect has been called the reasoning soul in Chapter 7; it is also called the intellectual (*noera*) soul, and, among other names, the "best part of the soul" (V.3.4, 13), and the "most divine part of soul" (V.3.9, 1): see Aubry 94n18. Plotinus, as often, is terminologically generous.

Our possession of the Forms is also twofold (lines 6–8), but here Plotinus is distinguishing between our intuitive and discursive cognition of them. Because Intellect is "a part of us" (13, 7–8 with Commentary 13, 5–8), we intuit it *qua* its content, the Forms, and these are intuited as a single whole corresponding to Intellect's unity. This unity, as often in Plotinus, is signalled by a tag from Anaxagoras, "all together" (*homou panta*, see Anaxagoras fr. B 1). Of the several occurrences of the tag in Plotinus (listed in HS_2, t. III, 327–328), most refer to Intellect/intelligibles, but the phrase is also applied to soul's unity (IV.2.2, 44; IV.4.11, 27; VI.4.14, 4 and 6) and to the unity of the visible world (V.8.9, 3). Anaxagoras' phrase refers to an original mixture of all the ingredients of the future universe, but this context is irrelevant to Plotinus, who may simply know the tag from Plato (*Gorgias* 465d4–5; *Phaedo* 72c3–5). It will have appealed to him because it suggests both the unity ("together," *homou*) and plurality (plural "all," *panta*) of intellect and soul. The broader, if flawed, awareness of Anaxagoras, fr. B 1 in II.4.7, 2–6 derives from Aristotle's polemical doxography (Armstrong 2.118n1). Plotinus will probably not have been aware that Anaxagoras' argument counters Parmenides' concept of the total unity of what there is, *homou pan* (fr. 8, 5), where "all" (*pan*) is singular: see Tornau 1998, 102–104, on VI.4.4, 24–25, where Plotinus cites Parmenides. Emilsson, commenting on this passage in Emilsson and Strange 2015, 141–142, argues that Plotinus may, or may also, have Parmenides' phrase in mind in passages where it is commonly assumed that Anaxagoras is his sole reference.

Plotinus contrasts this all-togetherness of the Forms in Intellect with their "unrolled . . . and separated" presence in our reasoning soul (lines 7–8). The metaphor "unrolled" (*aneiligmena*) most likely derives from the unwinding of the traditional book-roll (not fully superseded by the codex in Plotinus' days: see Grafton and Williams 2006, 10–12) in order to read its text (see LSJ, *anelissō* I). Soul's "reading" of specific Forms is discursive and temporally conditioned (hence "separated").

8, 8–10 *But how do we possess the God? . . . truly essence*: The One or Good is here called "God" (*theos*), as elsewhere in Plotinus (e.g., I.8.2, 25; VI.8. 19, 11; VI.9.9, 55; see Meijer 1992, 63–64). Plotinus' description of the One as "mounted" (*epochoumenon*) on Intellect and true Being echoes Numenius' account of the First God or Good "mounted (*epochoumenon*) joyfully upon Being" (fr. 2, 16 des Places). In III.6.5, 24–29 the soul in a body purified of gluttony and other excesses is said to "ride on it (the body) tranquilly (*ep' autou ocheisthai*)." In VI.7.5, 21–25 the higher soul is said to "ride" (*epocheitai*, line 24) upon the lower soul that uses the body directly. In all these cases the higher being or principle "rides" on the lower. This image expresses, in Blumenthal's term, the "supraposition" of one being or principle on another (Blumenthal 1971, 56n28). In VI.7.17, 34–36 Plotinus goes further than mere assertion of supraposition, saying that the first principle (the Good of the preceding chapters) "sits" (*epikathētai*) on "the . . . totality of things" (= Forms), "not that it may have a base but that it may base the 'Form' of the first 'Forms,' being formless itself" (trans. Armstrong). Aristotle's description of intellect (*nous*) as "form of forms" (*De Anima* III.8, 432a2) is alluded to here. The Good is supraposed on Intellect, but, rather than being supported by it, it supports Intellect, like (it has been suggested) a keystone at the summit of an arch: the supraposition image becomes complex and striking (on the difficulties of the VI.7.17 passage see Hadot 1987, 133–134n165, where the keystone analogy is suggested; Aubry 94n21).

8, 10–15 *and we are third . . . while being one*: The "we" has not been absent from this chapter: a first person plural verb is understood in its opening question, then "we have/possess" in lines 3 and 6, and this again understood in lines 8–9 in relation to the god/Good. In line 10 "we" (*hēmas*) explicitly situates the self at the third level of the hierarchy One/Good-Intellect-Soul. This contextualizes what Plotinus has argued in the preceding chapter: the "we" is the reasoning soul, "where we above all are" (7, 15–16 and 21–24). It may also suggest—*en passant* so to speak—our proximity to the highest principle, the "god" who is One and Good (see Aubry 243): "Since the soul is so valuable and divine a thing, straightway confident that such a thing will approach God, with such a principle go up towards him. Certainly you will not be shooting from a distance, nor will the intermediaries be many" (V.1.3, 1–4, trans. Atkinson).

Plotinus is not concerned here with the relation between hypostasis Soul, world-Soul, and individual souls. What interests him in this context is the link between his concept of soul in general (see Emilsson 2017, 265n7) and the soul-body theme of the treatise. He cites a phrase from Plato, *Timaeus* 35a in lines 11–12. It is a key text for him. He quotes or alludes to it in several treatises, in support of his account of the relation between soul and body (HS_2 III, 362). In the *Timaeus* it describes the composition of the world soul by the Demiurge. The passage reads: "Between the indivisible being that is always in the same state, *and the being that comes to be in bodies and is divisible* (*kai tēs au peri ta sōmata gignomenēs meristēs*), he mixed a third intermediate form of being from these two" (35a1–4). Plotinus (mis)understands the italicized words to mean "*the being that becomes divisible in bodies*" (see Tornau 1998, 18–21, commenting on VI.4.1, 2–3, where pre-Plotinian interpretations of *Timaeus* 35a are also briefly surveyed; Morelli 2011). His concern is to preserve the concept of soul as one eternal, unextended, indivisible being, pre-existing any embodiment, and at the same time to account for the presence of individual souls in separate individual extended bodies. Plotinus explores the problems that his view of the soul poses in a number of treatises: IV.1 and IV.2 (see Gurtler 2015, 299–343); and many chapters of IV.3–4 (see Dillon and Blumenthal 2015) and VI.4–5 (see Tornau 1998; Emilsson and Strange 2015).

In our treatise Plotinus focuses on one point: soul "divisible in bodies." He begins by observing (lines 13–15) that this is so, because soul is present in bodies, whatever their size—including the universe itself—while remaining one. Elsewhere he will refine this observation by calling the soul "one and many" (IV.2.2, 49–55) even prior to embodiment, and arguing that its divisibility is apparent rather than real, because it is everywhere as a whole in a given body, and not "parcelled out over the parts of the body" (VI.4.4, 32–33: for VI.4.4, 26–46 see Emilsson and Strange 2015, 142–143).

8, 15–18 *or in the sense that . . . a face in many mirrors*: Plotinus continues with a further observation on the "divisible in bodies" point. He adopts the refinement of VI.4.4, 26–46 (see preceding comment) that the divisibility of the soul is apparent, "imagined," and he links this to the argument of our treatise (7, 1–6) that it is not the soul that is present to bodies, but a soul-trace. He uses the same light metaphor (7, 4; 8, 15) in both passages. The soul itself "remains": the phrase is incomplete, suggesting that it remains one, or indivisible, or unchanged (all appropriate). It gives off "images" (*eidōla*), one of the terms he uses elsewhere for the soul-trace (see Commentary 7, 1–6). The mirror-image of lines 17–18 expresses the soul's oneness and its apparent multiple presence in many bodies. It is free of the moral overtones of another mirror motif, that of IV.3.12, 1–12, where the Orphic myth of the mirror of Dionysos alludes to soul's flawed descent or fall into body (see Dillon and Blumenthal 2015, 228–229). Plotinus will explore some implications of this latter theme in the following chapter of our treatise. There are other mirror images in Plotinus, some closer in tendency to our passage, like those of III.6 (chiefly in relation to the Receptacle in Plato's *Timaeus*) on matter's non-being and illusory "appearances" in it (III.6.7, 23–26: Fleet 1995, 175), and the no less illusory presence of the Forms in it (III.6.13, 34–55: Fleet 1995, 229–233). What is striking is the differentiated way in which Plotinus uses this imagery in each context (on mirror imagery in Plotinus see Ferwerda 1965, 9–23; for the wider context see Clark 2016, 83–90).

8, 18–23 *The first image is perception . . . toward what is produced*: Plotinus now briefly alludes to the range of faculties or powers of soul (see Commentary 3, 17–21), beginning with *aisthēsis,* which includes the faculty or "power of perception" (see 6, 9), an activity involving the "common entity" (*koinon*), as Chapters 6 and 7 have suggested (6, 12–14; 7, 3–6). But *aisthēsis* or *aisthētikon* often refers more generally to the sensitive faculty, which includes the five senses, common sense (see Commentary 9, 6–12), and consciousness (see Commentary 9, 15–23 and 11, 8–13), as well as imagination and memory (see the table in Blumenthal 1971, 44). A phrase from the *Timaeus* (69c7), "another kind (*eidos*) of soul," is generalized by Plotinus to refer to every other kind of soul (the phrase recurs later in our treatise, 12, 9 and 21).

In the *Timaeus* passage the reference is to the creation of the mortal soul, the embodied seat of the affections or passions, and of the irrational element. Plotinus extends the reference to all the lower powers of soul. He does not explicitly name the appetitive faculty, where affections and impulses are located (see Commentary 5, 3–7 and 5, 21–26), but he does name the lowest powers of reproduction and growth, the *phutikon* or vegetative faculty, which he elsewhere maintains that the body has directly from the world-soul (see Commentary 7, 1–6).

The final part of the sentence (lines 21–23) refers to the creative powers of soul generally, while specifying that this creative power involves "being turned toward (*epestrammenēs*)" what is produced. Elsewhere Plotinus exempts world-soul from "turning toward (*epistrophē*) the things here," whereas our souls "turn toward what requires care" (IV.3.4, 23 and 25, trans. Dillon and Blumenthal; see also IV.3.12, 11–12). Although Plotinus uses *epistrophē* and the related verb *epistrephein/–esthai* in a technical sense to denote the conversion of a lower level of being toward a higher prior level (Intellect turns toward the Good/One, soul turns toward Intellect and the Good; in 3, 23–26 above this conversion is philosophy's task), his use of the words in the present passage and in IV.3 to refer to the soul's "care" for its lower products shows that his terminology is not rigidly defined: *epistrophē* + genitive is idiomatic for "regard for, attention to." Soul's role is epitomized for Plotinus in Plato's "all soul cares for all that is soulless" (*Phaedrus* 246b6): these words introduce III.4.2, and lines 1–15 of that chapter stress the presence of all levels and faculties of soul in the living embodied human being. Plotinus' use of *epistrephesthai* in lines 22–23 refers exclusively to the soul's creative power, and carries no connotation of a flawed descent or decline of the soul into embodiment, but that is the other aspect of the soul's care that preoccupies him, and he will explore the moral risks involved in the soul's descent in Chapters 9 and 12 of our treatise.

Chapter 9

*Plotinus now turns overtly to the ethical implications of his psychology. If the soul, free from affections and impeccable, is thereby free from responsibility for what we do or suffer, then responsibility must lie with the fallible common entity (*koinon*). Much of the chapter discusses the reasoning soul, in particular its relation to Intellect, and its role in making judgments in perception. The account of the potential fallibility of opinion and reason takes up the question asked in 1, 7–8. The "we" continues to occupy Plotinus, and he introduces the related concept of consciousness, here to account for reason's apparently discontinuous actualization of intelligibles or Forms.*

9, 1–6 *So the nature of that soul . . . many evils are done because of it*: Plotinus has argued in the previous chapter that the soul does not descend into human bodies, but transmits "images" (*eidōla*, 8, 17) of itself into entities lower than itself. Now, turning to the moral implications of his theory, and in particular to issues of responsibility and the source of evil, he begins by asserting that this undescended soul is free from responsibility for the evil that we do or suffer (already a supposition of Chapter 2 of the treatise). These are the concern of the living thing, the "common" entity. He refers back ("as it has been described," lines 3–4) to earlier accounts of this entity, in particular to that of the "combination" in 7, 1–6 ("living thing," "common" entity, and "combination" are equivalent terms, as has become clear in the course of the treatise). But he must nonetheless face the problems that his theory poses. The soul as reasoning agent deals in opinions (see 7, 14–17), and these can be false, even harmful. How then is the soul "free from error" (*anamartētos*, lines 4–5)? Plotinus uses an adjective related to the term *hamartia* here, and also employs these and related terms later (8, 13; 11, 10; 12, 6), to refer to a wide spectrum that includes simple mistakes as well as moral faults.

Plotinus' phrase "the nature of that soul of ours" (line 1) may echo Aristotle's use of "nature" (*phusis*) to refer to something's essence, *De Anima* I.1, 402a7–10 (on which see Shields 2016, 83–85): see Commentary 7, 1–6.

9, 6–12 *Now evils are done . . . before the reasoning faculty passes judgment*: Plotinus will develop a more complex concept of the "we" or self in this and later chapters. In Chapter 7 he has located it in the reasoning soul that deals, among other things, with opinions (7, 14–17). But now he asserts that its range is wider ("we are many"), for he has to admit that the influence of the "worse"—whether affections (attributed to the "combination" in Chapter 7) or "an evil image"—overcomes *us*, and not something other than us ("evil image," *eidōlou kakou*: Tornau 330 emends, not implausibly, to *eidōlou kalou*, "a beautiful image," as in I.6.8, 9–10, referring to the Narcissus myth as a paradigm of the self-absorption with bodily beauty). He will return to the theme of the "we" in Chapter 11. The "worse" here refers to influences that can cause moral faults. But Plotinus (see comment on *hamartia* above, 9, 1–6) does not want to lose sight of a cause of other faults or mistakes, namely an "imagining" (*phantasia*) or representation that has not been subjected to reason's judgment. Acting on the basis of an unexamined "imagining" (e.g., an optical illusion) is due to another kind of influence of the "worse," for it entails that we accept the apparent data of sensation rather than referring them to reason's discernment. We are back with the account of sense-perception, and Plotinus is in this chapter more explicit than he was in Chapter 7 on the role of reason's judgment in perception.

What does "common perception" (*koinē aisthēsis*) refer to in line 12? Plotinus has identified the "common" entity (*to koinon*) as the faculty where perceptions occur, and it seems natural to understand "common perception" here to refer to the perceptions of this common entity, and so equivalent to "perception in the common entity" of 8, 18–19 (see Emilsson 1988, 166n37). But most commentators assume that Plotinus is referring here to Aristotle's "common sense" (or "common perception"), our perception of certain objects coincidentally by more than one of the five senses (e.g., motion, which is sometimes perceived simultaneously by touch and sight): *De Anima* II.6, 418a16–20 and III.1, 425a14–b3 (see Shields 2016, 226–227, 260–262). But, although Aristotle uses the term "common perception" (e.g., *De Anima* III.1, 425a27) alongside variant verbal forms when discussing this kind of perception, it is not an exclusive technical term for him, and need not be one for Plotinus. And why should Plotinus refer to the complex case of co-incidental perception here, when he is, in this passage, making general points about the common entity's perceptions?

9, 12–15 *The intellect is either in contact . . . not have it to hand*: In speaking of the Intellect being in contact with the reasoning soul Plotinus uses a verb (*ephaptesthai*) that he had already used earlier in the treatise to identify one of the possible soul-body relations, "a form in contact" (3, 20). This relation was illustrated by the craftsman and helmsman analogies, strong versions, for Plotinus, of the instrumentalist thesis, in which soul is essentially separate from the body it uses. Thus "in contact" in line 12 of the present passage is a code for "essentially separate." That is why, whether in contact with the reasoning soul or not, Intellect remains "free from error" (*anamartētos* again: see Commentary 9, 1–6). Plotinus immediately applies what could be called the "we" perspective to this: we are either in contact with Intellect *qua* object of our thinking, the *noēton* ("intelligible"), or not (here again "in contact" underlines the distinction between Intellect and reasoning soul). In a further shift of perspective, Plotinus talks of the intelligible "in us." This refers back to the discussion of Chapter 8, on the ways in which Intellect is ours, and adds to it the assertion that we have Intellect *qua* intelligible, but do not always have it "to hand" (*procheiron*), that is, we may be conscious of having it or not. There is a reminiscence here of Plato, *Theaetetus* 198d (the term *procheiron* occurs in d7), where Plato is attempting to account for regaining knowledge of things previously acquired but not "ready to hand" in our thought. Plotinus refers later in the chapter (line 20) to reason's consciously seeing forms, applying one of his most fruitful insights, the role of consciousness, to the issue under discussion (see Commentary 9, 15–23).

9, 15–23 *So then, we have distinguished . . . what is outside and what is within*: Plotinus' distinction between "common" and "peculiar" here echoes Aristotle, *De Anima* I.1, 403a3–5, which distinguishes between "affections (*pathē*) of the soul . . . whether all are common to what has the soul as well or whether there is something peculiar to the soul itself" (trans. Shields). The former refers to affections common to body and soul. It should be noted that Aristotle is using the term "affections" here to refer, not merely to the passions, but also to perception and reasoning (Shields 2016, 95). Plotinus intends a similar range of activities, and with "common" he is clearly referring to those of the common entity, specified at 7, 5–6 as including perception and the living thing's affections. He further distinguishes here between bodily attributes and activities, and those not without body, presumably a distinction between purely corporeal states (such as, for instance, having freckles), and those requiring body, but also entailing some kind of soul-trace (such as affections). What, on the other hand, does not require body for its actualization or activation (*energeia*) is peculiar to the reasoning soul: Plotinus gives the example of reason's judgment exercised on the impressions (*tupoi*) produced from sensation, but apprehended as intelligibles (see 7, 9–12: on these impressions see Commentary 7, 6–16). The present chapter reiterates conclusions of Chapter 7, including the assertion that the reasoning soul in its judgment role in perception is "already seeing forms" (19–20): see 7, 12 ("these impressions are already intelligibles") and 13–14 ("a contemplation of forms alone"). But Plotinus also adds new elements to the account. Having alluded to consciousness in line 15 (see Commentary 9, 12–15), he now refers explicitly to it in line 20: reason sees forms consciously, that is, activated in our apprehension of them.

A key text on consciousness and the unconscious in Plotinus is I.4.9–10, on which see McGroarty 2006, 138–161 (here 140n6 further literature on the topic: see especially Schwyzer 1960, Warren 1964, Dodds 1973, 135–136, Schroeder 1987, Gurtler 1988, 49–90).

The reading *sunaisthēsei* ("consciously"), found in some manuscripts, follows HS and modern editors (Igal,

Armstrong), but Aubry 98n39 argues for *sun aisthēsei*, "with sensation," the reading of several manuscripts, which would stress the concomitant roles of sensation and intellectual apprehension in perception. This interpretation gets some support from the reference in lines 22–23 to likeness and commonality between the external and internal in perception (see below). For a different interpretation of the passage, understanding *sunaisthēsei* to refer to "sympathy," see Emilsson 2017, 279–280.

The "proper reasoning" and "true soul" references in lines 20–21 must refer to the reasoning soul and its discursive thinking (*dianoia*, 21): the soul is "true" in that it is distinct from the soul-trace in the combination. The "true reasoning" (line 22) of the soul is the activation or actualization of "intellections" (*noēseis*, line 21), that is, of the Forms in it *qua* intellectual soul. The emphasis on "true" highlights the grounding of the undescended soul's thinking and its avoidance of erroneous opinions in its possession of the Forms. Plotinus is reiterating what he has argued in the preceding Chapters 7 and 8, as well as in lines 12–15 of this chapter (see Commentary 9, 12–15). He adds here that this reasoning of soul is often accompanied by "a likeness (*homoiotēs*) and community (*koinōnia*)" between the external and the internal (lines 22–23). This is most likely a reference to the way in which perception functions. In the key chapter IV.4.23 on perception (for a summary of it see Commentary 7, 6–16) Plotinus posits a necessary mediating entity that enables the soul to apprehend external sense-objects and says that "it must share the affections (*sumpathes*) of the objects and have similar affections (*homoiopathes*)," IV.4.23, 21–22 (trans. Dillon and Blumenthal). This sympathy between our perceptive powers and sense-objects, as well as the general sympathy of the various parts of the cosmos (a living, ensouled thing), enable perception to occur (Blumenthal 1971, 76–78, 136–137). IV.5 proposes a complex account of vision that refines this concept of sympathy (see Gurtler 2015, 16–18, 22–23, and, for a detailed commentary, 230–297; important discussion also in Emilsson 1988, 47–62).

9, 23–26 *So the soul will . . . whatever this is*: Plotinus reiterates his concept of the unchanging soul, free from affections and disturbances of any kind, and adds to it his view of the soul's self–reflexion, its "internal" concentration upon itself *qua* reasoning soul. The phrase "in itself" may echo Plato, *Republic* 589a7–b1, "the man within," formulated in a context where Plato is contrasting the rational and other parts of the soul (*Republic* 588c–590b). There are quotations from, and an exegesis of, the Plato passage in Chapter 7 (see Commentary 7, 18–24). Change, on the other hand, is an effect of the affections of the common entity, and "what has become attached." This latter must refer to the body that, with the soul-trace, forms the common entity, especially as Plotinus refers ("as has been described") to an earlier discussion, no doubt that of Chapter 7 (see Commentary 7, 1–6). Plotinus uses the same verb (*sunartasthai*) at VI.8.15, 15 to refer to what has become attached to us and makes us subject to chance, and not master of ourselves. The "tumult" (*thorubos*) in the soul as a consequence of embodiment may, as HS point out, echo Plato's use of the term in similar contexts (*Phaedo* 66d6, *Timaeus* 43b6); Pradeau 2010, 227–228, plausibly suggests the influence of *Phaedrus* 248a–b.

Plotinus' reference to the common entity in lines 25–26 is qualified by the phrase "whatever this is." This seems surprising, given that Plotinus has given a clear account of it in Chapter 7 and added details in Chapter 8 and the present chapter. Perhaps he is simply preparing the reader for further discussion in Chapters 10–12, where he applies the account of the common entity (or composite, 11, 1) to specific, not unproblematic issues—relation to the "we" (once again), the cases of children and animals, continuing concerns about wrongdoing and responsibility in relation to the soul. These add precision to his account. Thus Armstrong has "whatever precisely that is" (likewise Tornau 321).

Chapter 10

This chapter develops the ethical discussion of the previous chapter. Plotinus continues to make distinctions between the unaffected reasoning soul and the common entity. The concept of a dual "we" or self is introduced, corresponding to this distinction. The theory of two kinds of virtue is a further consequence. The themes of the soul's survival after death (further discussed in Chapter 12) and of friendship are briefly considered.

10, 1–5 *But if we are the soul . . . we say too that it affects us*: In 7, 14–16 Plotinus has asserted that it is precisely at the level of the reasoning, discursive soul that the "we" is pre-eminently situated. In 7, 18–24 this reasoning soul is called the "true man" and, again, the "we." In 9, 23–24 he has stressed the unchanging nature of soul, its freedom from affections and its self-reflexion, with, as in Chapter 7, echoes of Plato's "inner man" theme (see notes on 7, 18–24 and 9, 23–26). Now, with another Platonic allusion, this time to *Alcibiades* 130c (man is the ruling soul: see Commentary 1, 2–4), he returns to the problem of the unaffected soul, appealing at once to common sense and to the way we talk of affections. We are affected by passions and changes, and we are agents: how can the soul not be affected, or not be the agent, if we are the soul? To prepare an answer, Plotinus concentrates on the "we." He reminds us that the common entity has been said to be ours in our bodily condition: what affects the body affects us. He is referring here to 7, 6–9 and probably also to 9, 6–8.

10, 5–7 *So the "we" is double . . . endowed with life*: In 9, 7 Plotinus has observed that we are manifold beings. Now, as in a number of other passages, he says that we are twofold. He makes "we" a substantive by prefixing the definite article (*to hēmeis*), "the we," thereby stressing its function as a key concept in his argument. Here the "we" is double (*ditton*) because it can either include the "animal (*thērion*)," defined as the living body (and therefore the same as the common entity), or simply refer to the superior reasoning soul. The former is sometimes called the empirical self in modern discussions (Remes 2007, 10–15—and throughout—calls it the embodied self; O'Daly 1973 often calls it the historical self). Why "animal"? Most likely because the word occurs at 7, 21 in the quotation from Plato's *Republic* 588c7, used there by Plotinus to characterize the irrational element in humans. Its use here functions as a reference to that earlier passage. Of the other texts that talk of us as double, II.3.9, 30–31 is closest to the passage under discussion: "each one is double, on the one hand a kind of combination (*sunamphoteron*), on the other himself (*autos*)." Here as elsewhere *autos* can refer to the self or "we," as in "the soul is the self" (*hē psuchē autos*, IV.7.1, 24–25: on this use of *autos* see Henry 1960, 448; Fleet 2016, 76–78 and 83–84). Even when we have attained the moral perfection of the sage; we are still dual beings: "such a man would be god and spirit (*daimōn*), being double (*diplous*), or rather having with him someone else with another kind of virtue" (I.2.6, 4–6). In a discussion of memory and imagination and of the difficulty of attributing these to the reasoning soul or the irrational element in IV.3 (where the latter is identified as a second soul), Plotinus says that "in general the duality (*to ditton*) of the souls escapes our notice" (IV.3.31, 15, trans. Dillon and Blumenthal), suggesting that our sense of this duality is not intuitive, but rather a result of analysis.

10, 7–11 *But the true man is other . . . following along with it*: The "true man" has already been referred to at 7, 20: there, as here (line 7), the term denotes the reasoning soul, as do the references to the "true soul" and "true reasoning" in 9, 21–22 (for the emphasis on "true" see Commentary 9, 15–23). This man is "pure" (*katharos*) of things bodily (Plotinus is not explicit about what "these things" refers to, and translators often supply "affections": but Plotinus has just been talking about the "we" and the living body), having virtues that Plotinus says here are "in intellection (*noēsei*)." The allusion to "pure" points to what he calls the cathartic virtues in I.2, in a version of the four cardinal virtues which entails detachment from the body, whereby "the soul acts alone—this is intelligence and wisdom—and does not share the body's experiences—this is self-control—and is not afraid of departing from the body—this is courage—and is ruled by reason (*logos*) and intellect (*nous*), without opposition—and this is justice" (I.2.3, 15–19, trans. Armstrong; on I.2 see Dillon 1983, 92–102). The notions of purification and separation from the body as the goal of philosophy are preeminently Platonic (*Phaedo* 67c–d) and have been already invoked by Plotinus in Chapter 3 (see Commentary 3, 11–17 and 17–21, where the possible influence of Aristotle's views on separation is also considered). Here the soul in which the higher virtues reside is said to be "separating (*chōrizomenē(i)*) and separate (*chōristē(i)*)" (line 9). The first term here must be in the middle voice (hence the translation "separating") as passivity cannot be attributed to the soul: it is active in sense, perhaps reflexive, and may therefore mean "separating itself," denoting what the soul must do to realize detachment from things temporal and bodily. But the soul is, in fact, ontologically "separate," as the second term of the phrase indicates. So the phrase combines allusion to the inextricably linked moral and ontological aspects of separation for the Platonist Plotinus.

The further "departure" referred to in lines 10–11 must be death: Plotinus asserts that the soul-trace (here also "soul," i.e., the lower soul, as often in Plotinus), "illuminated" by the separate soul (see 7, 3–5 and Commentary 7, 1–6), must also depart with it. This introduces a topic to which Plotinus returns in detail in Chapter 12, the soul's survival after death.

10, 11–14 *But the virtues . . . jealousy and pity do*: Plotinus now turns to the other category of virtues, those acquired in the course of our lives, with an allusion to Plato, *Republic* VII, 518e1–2 ("virtues that really aren't there beforehand but are added later by habit and practice," trans. Grube and Reeve in Cooper 1997, 1136). There may also be an allusion to *Phaedo* 82b2, where there is talk of virtue "developed by habit and practice": this kind of virtue is "popular and civic (*politikēn*)" (*Phaedo* 82a11–b1). These are the civic virtues (*politikai aretai*) of Plotinus I.2, which "set us in order and make us better by giving limit and measure to our desires . . . and they abolish false opinions" (I.2.2, 14–17, trans. Armstrong). These virtues are called "civic" because they are involved in our social dealings with our fellow human beings. They order the appetitive, fallible part of the soul, and so are virtues of the common entity (line 13 in the current chapter), the seat of the affections (7, 4–6). In *Phaedo* 82b2–3 these virtues are said to develop "without philosophy or understanding (*nous*)"; in the *Republic* passage just referred to, the practical virtues are contrasted with "the virtue of reason" (*tou phronēsai*, 518e2). Likewise, in our chapter they are not produced "by reason (*phronēsis*, line 12)," that is, they do not entail philosophical thinking and the knowledge that derives from it. The terms *nous/noēsis* and *phronēsis* are paired in I.8.9, 2 and 15, 7–8, where "intellect/intellection" and "reason" are likely meanings (the pairing there echoing the *nous/phronēsis* pair that occurs several times in Plato's *Philebus*: see O'Meara 1999, 159, who, however, translates *phronēsis* by "wisdom").

As with the practical virtues, the vices are also those of the common entity (lines 13–14): the three named vices here (envy, jealousy, and pity) are found in Stoic lists of types of mental distress (*lupē*): see LS §65E = SVF III 394. Like the Stoics, Plotinus, who does not refer elsewhere to *eleos*, "pity," must be regarding it here as a disturbing emotion from which the sage should be free (see Sandbach 1975, 61–62). Aristotle includes pity among the passions (*Nicomachean Ethics* II.5, 1105b23), but says that involuntary behaviour excites pity, as well as pardon (*Nicomachean Ethics* III.1, 1109b31–32 and 1110b28–1111a2). In this he is consistent with a widespread ancient Greek view that compassion and forgiveness are appropriate reactions in certain circumstances (see Dover 1974, 195–201, where it is pointed out that *eleos* does not always denote a feeling or mental state). Pity in Plotinus: see Ferwerda 1984. On friendship and sympathy see further in the following lines and Commentary 10, 14–15). On the plural forms used here for the individual vices see 1, 1–2 with Commentary.

In line 13 there is an idiomatic inversion: the *kai* in *epei kai* is semantically part of the main clause (see Denniston 296–297 for this much-used idiom), hence my translation "the vices also." Beutler, perhaps sensing this, inserted a *kai* in the main clause (HBT Va, 292), but that is not necessary.

10, 14–15 *And what do friendships . . . the inner man*: Plotinus distinguishes between two kinds of *philia* (translated by "friendship," but the Greek word can cover a range of affectionate relationships—for partners, family, friends—that would be correctly rendered as "love" (Dover 1974, 212). One kind of *philia* is seated in the common entity, the other is "the inner man's." The latter phrase cites Plato, *Republic* 589a7–b1, part of a key text for Plotinus, as his exegesis of it in Chapter 7 has shown (see Commentary 7, 18–24). The "inner man," like the "true man" (7, 20 and 10,7), the "true soul" (9, 21), and "true reasoning" (9, 22), are codes for the unaffected reasoning soul. Plotinus (whose other references to friendship are brief but revealing: see below), never develops this distinction, but it most likely has similarities with Aristotle's distinction in *Nicomachean Ethics* VIII and IX between what John Cooper has called "virtue-friendship"—the perfect friendship of those who are good and mutually recognize their moral goodness—and friendship that is based on pleasure, or on advantage and utility (Cooper 1980, 303–308). When Plotinus does refer to friendship, he characterizes the attitude of the wise or good man (*spoudaios*) as not "unfriendly or hardhearted . . . rendering to his friends as much as he renders to himself, he will really be a friend because of his union with *Nous* (Intellect)" (I.4.15, 21–25, trans. McGroarty). Stoic and Epicurean views on friendship (see LS 137–138, 376; Sharples 1996, 118–124) may play a role here (see on this Plotinus text McGroarty 2006, 193–195). In IV.9.3, 1–4 Plotinus argues that the unity-in-multiplicity of all souls enables us to empathize with, enjoy, and be naturally attracted to our friends. Love (the more appropriate translation of *philia* here) in our world, being between separate things (or beings), is an imitation of the Love in Intellect, where there is unity in division (VI.7.14, 18–23): Plotinus is alluding here to Empedocles' universal Love principle (see KRS 287–308, 314–321), adapting it to a Platonist context. As in the I.4 passage, the metaphysics of love/friendship, so to speak, is grounded in the unity of Intellect, and in our union with it.

Chapter 11

Plotinus now shows how his concept of the living thing or common entity and its relation to reasoning soul can applied to the different cases of children and animals, develops his theory of consciousness beyond what has been said in Chapter 9, and extends the ethical considerations of Chapters 9 and 10 by considering the implications of the Pythagorean-Platonic theme that human souls can transmigrate into animals, and that this can be a punishment for flawed human lives. Here again he is concerned to relate his argument to his concept of the living thing and the undescended, separate soul. The chapter, though brief, is rich in aperçus *and argument. Aubry 307 suggests that it is the heart of the treatise, revealing how some of its basic questions can be answered, and how some of its fundamental insights function.*

11, 1–4 *When we are children . . . the middle <part>*: These lines are cryptic and difficult to interpret. Plotinus speaks of *ta anō* ("the things above," 2) and *to anō* ("what is above," 3), and, although these could refer to the same thing, there is good reason to believe that they do not. In addition, in the second and third sentences the subject is not expressed: what is it? and is it the same in each phrase? To begin at the beginning: the first sentence makes an uncomplicated statement about children. What comes from the "composite" (*suntheton*)—the term refers to the same as the "combination" and the "common" entity—is active in children, whereas "the things above" have little influence on them. Plotinus uses the same light metaphor to evoke the influence of "the things above" that he had used in 7, 3–4 to describe the genesis of the combination from a soul-trace, called "some kind of light given" by the soul, and the body. We can therefore assume that in the text under discussion what little light there is shines from the undescended, discursively reasoning soul, minimally active in young children. Plotinus uses a plural form, "the things above," to refer to the undescended soul, but it (quite naturally in Greek) has a singular reference. And this must be the unexpressed subject of the second sentence, which is an explanatory addition to to the first: that which is inactive in relation to us is active towards "what is above <it>." Plotinus is reiterating here the principle that, at each level of the hierarchy of being, the lower continuously turns or "converts" towards the higher being, that is, that soul is continuously turned towards Intellect, and Intellect towards the Good or One. In II.9.2, 4–6 one power of our soul is said to be continuously directed towards Intellect and the intelligibles, another power to the things here and now, and another power is in the middle between these. For "in the middle" see the passage from V.3 quoted below and the *meson* of the present chapter, lines 4 and 6; see also V.1.12, quoted and discussed below on 11, 4–8.

We must assume continuous conversion of soul towards Intellect in the present text also: "when it is inactive towards us" does not preclude conversion when it is active towards us.

So far so good. But what is the subject of the third sentence? To answer this considerations of syntax are less helpful than recognizing the particular philosophical point made here by Plotinus. What is it that reaches "the middle" (*meson*), and what is this middle? The answer is found in an earlier treatise, V.3 [49] (on this treatise see Beierwaltes 1991; Ham 2000). There Plotinus says that "it is we ourselves (*autoi*) who reason and we ourselves think the intelligibles (*nooumen ta . . . noēmata*) in discursive reasoning; for this is what we are. But the activities of Intellect are from above (*anōthen*) in the same way that those of sense-perception are from below; we are this, the principal part (*kurion*) of the soul, in the middle (*meson*) between two powers, a worse and a better, the worse that of sense-perception, the better that of Intellect" (V.3.3, 35–40, trans. Armstrong, modified). Applied to the present chapter, the quoted passage necessitates that the "middle" there refers to the same thing as the "middle" in our text, that is, both refer to the "principal part" of the soul, discursive reasoning soul (called the "first soul" in 8, 6 and the "true soul" in 9, 21). This latter cannot therefore be the subject of the third sentence. Again with reference to the V.3 passage, the subject must be Intellect, acting "from above." In the second sentence *to anō* (line 3) = Intellect must therefore be understood to be the subject of the third sentence: "And **it** (= *to anō* = Intellect) is active . . .". In the absence of a word like "this," the third sentence is difficult to construe. But there seems to be no alternative to assuming a change of subject in it. And the following lines 4–8 corroborate this interpretation.

Plotinus rarely refers to children's souls as he does here in lines 1–2. In III.1.7, 15–20, arguing against the Stoic chain of causation, he suggests that if our impulses are always determined by pre-existing causes we would be like animals and infants and the insane, acting on "blind impulses." In IV.6.3, 19–25 he argues that children are said to be better at remembering because they focus on physical, especially visual, appearances, and on a small number of these, whereas those in whom reason is active, "rush past" these appearances and do not always retain memories of them. In II.9. 17, 52 he observes that the universe has never been incomplete, as children are. This cryptic observation provides the clue to the source of his no less cryptic observation in the present chapter. The source is Plato's *Timaeus*. There, referring both to the first insertion of souls into bodies but also to the souls of all infants, the soul is said to be in a turbulent state, lacking intelligence (*anous*, 44a8) at first (44a–c). But the world-soul, by contrast, has unceasing intelligent life from the beginning (36e). It is this view of the development of intelligence as the infant and child grow towards adulthood that Plotinus refers to in the text under discussion, relating it to the ongoing discussion of the composite or common entity in the treatise, and adapting it to his view of the undescended soul.

11, 4–8 *What? Are we not also . . . disposition to actuality*: Plotinus now links his argument of the previous lines to his theories of the self and consciousness, both of which have been deployed in the preceding chapters (see Commentary 7, 16–18; 8, 10–15; 9, 6–12; 9, 12–15; 9, 15–23;10, 1–5; 10, 5–7). His first question is: are we not also Intellect? His earlier statements have asserted that we have total access to transcendent Intellect (8, 1–8), and that we are in contact with the intelligible in Intellect and in us (9, 13–15). In both these passages, "we" is equivalent to the reasoning soul. In Chapter 10 he introduces the concept of the double "we," and there again the "true man," the higher level of self, is the reasoning soul (10, 7–10). His question in the present chapter and its implicit answer suggests a wider range for the "we," multiple rather than double, including the level of Intellect. The answer here is implicit. "But there must be conscious awareness (*antilēpsis*)" seems to posit the condition whereby we are, in whatever sense, Intellect. At the end of the treatise, Plotinus asserts that Intellect "too is a part of us," and this conclusion seems unavoidable in the light of what he has argued in 8, 1–8 and the present passage (see Tornau 431

n. 56). Plotinus has already identified the "we" as Intellect in VI.5.7, 3–6, arguing that we think the intelligibles "by being them . . . if we participate in true knowledge, we are those objects, not by taking them into ourselves, but rather by ourselves being in them" (trans. Emilsson and Strange). Here Plotinus is applying Aristotle's view that pure intellection entails that the thinking subject is identical with its object. But Plotinus goes further, as Emilsson observes: "the self is one of the intelligibles, not just a tourist inspecting this realm from an external point of view" (Emilsson and Strange 2015, 242). Another text corroborates this view: "we understand ourselves best when we have made our self-knowledge one with ourselves (*tēn epistēmēn hēmōn kai hēmas ēn pepoiēkotes*). In the higher world . . . our knowledge is most perfectly conformed to Intellect (*kata noun*)" (V.8.11, 31–34, trans. Armstrong). There is an apparent contradiction between these texts and V.3.3, 31–32. There Plotinus asserts that "we are not Intellect," but that we use it intermittently, without becoming it: "we are conformed to it (*kat' ekeinon*)." The same idea of being conformed to Intellect occurs in the text just quoted from V.8.11.

So does Plotinus contradict himself? In V.3.3 Plotinus is intent on firmly locating the self at the level of discursive reason. This is clear from the passage quoted above (see Commentary 11, 1–4). At the same time he maintains that, even if "Intellect is our king," "we too are kings, when we are in accord with it," and one way of being in accord with

Intellect entails "being as if filled with it and able to see it and be aware of it as present" (V.3.3, 45 – 4, 4, trans. Armstrong). It is, as VI.5.7 has argued, no mere knowledge of something external. Nevertheless, the argument of V.3.3 (on which see Ham 2000, 111–122) apparently says something different from what Plotinus seems to maintain in VI.5.7 and the present text. One cannot argue that Plotinus' thought has developed on this point, for V.3 [49] was written in the period between VI.4–5 [22–23] and our treatise. The most likely explanation for the apparent difference is that in V.3 Plotinus is concerned to tie the concept of the "we" to the discursively reasoning soul. Even if intellection entails that we are one with the objects of our thought, we are not pure Intellect. There is an essential difference between what we are and what Intellect is. At the same time, our intellection is not that of another: it is ours. The concept of the "we" expresses this. Plotinus, one might say, prefers the apparent contradiction in these texts to a clear-cut distinction between "we" and Intellect that would undermine the, for him, undeniable subjective dimension of our intellection.

In V.3.3, 27–29 Plotinus stresses that "we use it <sc. Intellect> and do not use it .. and it is ours when we use it, but not ours when we do not use it" (trans. Armstrong). He is asserting there what he repeats in our text. There must be "apprehension (*antilēpsis*)" of Intellect, and this happens when we direct the "middle," our discursive reason, towards "what is above" (here Intellect again). The role of conscious focusing is again stressed in these texts. The argument in both is identical: there is no contradiction between them. Two further texts, both early (V.1 [10] 12 and IV.8 [6] 8), are worth adducing here. In V.1.12 Plotinus asks how one can possess the hypostases without being aware that one does so. His approach to the answer is the same as in the texts just discussed. "Not everything which is in soul is immediately perceptible (*aisthēton*), but it reaches 'us' only when it reaches perception (*aisthēsin*). . . each of the parts of the soul lives continually and is active continually in its own independent activity, but there is recognition only when communication and apprehension (*antilēpsis*) take place" (V.1.12, 5–12, trans. Atkinson, modified). Plotinus' use of the terms *aisthēton* and *aisthēsis* here must refer to consciousness, to a conscious perception that is not reducible to sense-perception (but for a different view see Atkinson 1985, 244–246, Tornau 356 n. 78). One cannot "perceive" Intellect or the Good through sense-perception.

Toward the end of V.1.12 Plotinus urges us to turn inwards, so as "to hear the sounds from above (*anō*)," lines 20–21). His use of the code word "above" (*anō*) has the same function as in the present chapter. In IV.8.8 there is a similar argument, with, as Atkinson 1985, 244–245 has observed, similar language used. Here again Plotinus' loose use of *aisthēsis* and related terms is evident, and once again the sense of *aisthēsis* in lines 5 and 6–7 must be "consciousness" rather than sense-perception. In the later IV.3 [27] 30

Plotinus develops a theory of imagination (*phantasia*) which stores memories of intellections as well as (in parallel manner) of sense-perceptions, and he identifies "apprehension" (*antilēpsis*), a term for conscious awareness (as in our chapter), with the imagination. There is a similar argument in I.4.10, which states explicitly the parallelism of the imaging of intellections and of sense-perception (see lines 10–16 there).

To return to the present chapter. In lines 5–8 the role of the reasoning soul, our "middle," as the agent of our actions is stressed. It is not merely a conscious recipient of intellections or sense-perceptions, but also a moral agent, directing us "above" or in the opposite direction, towards the better or the worse. There is a third activity mentioned in the final part of the sentence, but it is less an alternative to the other two and more a generic assertion of the role of our reasoning soul in all our deliberate actions, viewed here in Aristotelian terms as the actualization of a capacity (*dunamis*) or disposition (*hexis*). Aubry 101 n. 61 cites a number of different interpretations of this text.

11, 8–13 *But how does the living thing . . . an image of soul*: Plotinus' question about how the living thing includes animals (i.e. non-human animals) is answered by distinguishing between animals into which a human soul has migrated (the present section) and natural animal lives (lines 13–15). His reference to punitive transmigration of human souls into animals is first and foremost a reference to this theme in a number of Plato's dialogues: *Phaedrus* 248–249, *Phaedo*

81–82, *Republic* 620 (where there is a choice of animal lives, and not necessarily a punitive one), *Timaeus* 42 and 91–92 (where animals are first created from flawed humans). But Plotinus will have known that Empedocles believed in punitive reincarnation cycles (KRS 314–317) and Pythagoras in transmigration into animal forms (KRS 219–220). That may be one reason why he does not identify his source by name ("as is said," line 9). But he often refers to "the ancients" when Plato is meant (e.g. IV.3.23, 24), or to other philosophers without naming them (Aristotle in the present treatise, 4, 26), or, in the case of transmigration into animal bodies, to "those who in ancient times have philosophised best about the soul" (VI.4.16, 4–5, trans. Armstrong). As Tornau 1998, 300 suggests, this may because on this particular topic, apart from the earlier authority of Pythagoras on transmigration—and Plotinus' tendency to find anticipations of Plato's teachings in earlier philosophers (IV.8.1; V.1.8–9)—Plato himself stresses the antiquity or exotic provenance of the sources for his myths (*Phaedrus* 235b–c, *Republic* 614b). Assessing Plato's purpose in his eschatological or other myths is not easy, but neither can his personal recasting of myths be dismissed: at the very least they have a moral message, imaginatively presented (Rutherford 1995, 171–178, 215–218, 257–260, 309–312). On the other hand, later Platonists had difficulties with, or dismissed, the notion of human transmigration into animal bodies (see Dörrie 1957).

As for Plotinus' attitude to the animal transmigration theory (see Rich 1957; Stamatellos 2013; Kalligas 2014, 127–128; Fleet 2016, 291–295, commenting on IV.7.14, 1–8), he is concerned enough about it to stress that it is, or should be, consistent with his own psychology. In VI.4.16, 6–7 (where he is referring not just to transmigration, but to soul's descent and ascent, and judgments of it) he says that "it is proper to try to show that our present discourse is in agreement, or at least not in disagreement with" (trans. Armstrong) ancient authorities. In VI.7.6, 21–23 he asks how a human soul can assume an animal body when it is the forming principle (*logos*) of human beings, and answers, alluding to his view that all souls are one, that the soul is "all things, but is active at different times in accordance with a different <forming principle>" (trans. Armstrong, modified). A soul forming an animal is therefore, forming something less valuable than a human, but not something unnatural for it (VI.7.7, 1–5). At III.4.2 he speculates, as Plato does, about the appropriate animals for the souls whose previous existence has been imperfect, and seems to enjoy doing so (stupid kings become eagles, if stupidity was their sole fault; unphilosophic astronomers become high-flying birds, lines 25–28). In the present passage he adapts the theory to what he has previously said about the living thing and the soul-trace or image in it (7, 1–6 with Commentary). The reasoning soul does not descend into the animal body any more than it does into the human body. The animal's consciousness (*sunaisthēsis*, line 11) is of the soul-image with the body—and, one can add, is limited to that: the animal cannot exercise the reasoning powers of the undescended human soul.

Behind this view lies Plotinus' doctrine that whatever is received and activated by bodies depends on the capacity of the particular recipient body (see Emilsson and Strange 2015, 26–28; Lee 1979). But the embodied soul-image will allow it to experience sensations and other affections, and to have impulses and an appropriate kind of memory. The "body of such a kind" (line 12) repeats 7, 3 (see Commentary 7, 1–6). The statement that the separate soul "being present, is not present" to animals (line 11) repeats the paradoxical turn of phrase of IV.3.22, 3, where Plotinus is speculating that soul might be present to body as fire is to air (i.e. "the light from the fire is present *to* the air, but not mixed in it," Dillon and Blumenthal 2015, 270). Similar phrases are found in two passages in III.6: in 1, 36–37 ("the soul possesses without possessing and is affected without being affected") and 2, 39–44 ("<the reasoning part> possesses what it sees <in Intellect>—yet does not possess it," trans. Fleet, modified). In the first of these passages Plotinus is saying that one can only talk of the rational soul having irrational affections by analogy, 1, 35. In the second passage he is saying that the soul does not possess what it intelligizes (in the sense of storing it, as if it were like an imprint in wax), but exercises its rational power of discerning (*ginōskein*) and, by analogy with sight, "approaches that to which it is essentially related and is it by knowing, and discerns without being affected" (2, 36–37, trans. Fleet: on 2, 34–44 see Fleet 1995, 96–99). In all these passages, including the present chapter, Plotinus is concerned to maintain the impossibility of the soul being affected by anything lower or higher than it on the scale of beings.

If the animal to which a human soul has been assigned has no awareness of the soul's reasoning powers, in what does the punishment of transmigration into an animal body consist? Is the reasoning soul aware of the transmigration, even if the animal is not? These are questions that Plotinus does not appear to consider.

11, 13–15 *But if a human soul . . . has come into being*: Where no human soul is linked to the animal life, then the animal *qua* living thing is ensouled by illumination from "universal soul" (here referring to the world-soul: Aubry 102n65). This is also how the human soul's lowest powers of reproduction and growth are acquired (see 8, 20–21 and Commentary 7, 1–6 and 8, 18–23). The distinction between two kinds of animal souls corresponds to that of IV.7.14, 1–5, where "living nature" (here, as in IV.4.18, 2–4, the lowest power of world-soul) is the source of the second kind. But what about the animal's powers of sensation, memory, and the affections generally? Will illumination from the world-soul enable these also? Again, Plotinus does not consider these questions. Caluori 2015, 195 reports Eyjólfur Emilsson's suggestion that Plotinus may be distinguishing in this chapter between species of animals who have higher souls (e.g., monkeys), and those who do (and can) not (e.g., flies).

Chapter 12

In a complex chapter Plotinus continues to be puzzled by the concept of afterlife rewards and punishments, wrestles with Platonic texts (and Plato's apparent view that the soul is a composite entity) on this topic, and attempts to develop his own position, which relies in the end on some of these same Platonic texts. The question of the survival of the soul-trace after death is discussed, and different answers are given, depending on whether the individual is a philosopher or not. In this context the implications of Herakles' dual posthumous existence in Homer are explored.

12, 1–5 *But if the soul is faultless . . . how they are not in conflict*: Despite, or perhaps precisely because of, his arguments for a flawless soul, Plotinus is concerned to explain how there can be "judgments" after death. The word in line 1 translated "judgments" is *dikai*, which can mean "punishments," but the mention of the soul "acting rightly" in line 3 indicates that Plotinus is also thinking of rewards. His concern here has above all to do with Plato's repeated assertions in the eschatological myths in several dialogues that human souls are judged, and rewarded or punished, after death. Lines 4–5 suggest that he may be trying to reconcile Plato's views with his own, and that would be consistent with his Plato exegesis in general. It is, however, debatable whether such reconciliation is achieved, or even possible, in this chapter.

Plotinus has two Platonic texts in mind. One, *Republic* 611b–612a, will be cited in lines 11–17 of the chapter; the other, *Phaedo* 80c–84b, has played a role in the previous chapter (see Commentary 11, 8–13), and, although it is not explicitly referred to here, it is undoubtedly influential. Brief consideration of the themes of these two passages will provide the context of Plotinus' argument.

In the *Phaedo* passage, the soul, the invisible part of a human being, is imagined to pass into the invisible region of Hades (Plato alludes in *Phaedo* 80d to an etymology of "Hades" as "the invisible": Plotinus refers to this etymology in VI.4.16, 36–37: on this passage see Commentary on 12, 20–31 and 31–39). If the soul is in a pure state on account of its philosophical detachment from bodily things during its life, it will find eternal happiness in the invisible realm. This pure soul has an affinity with the divine, and is described as having "gathered itself together to be by itself" (80e) in life and being "alone by itself" in the afterlife (81c). But the soul that has been obsessed with, and dominated by, what is bodily, will be dragged back (apparently immediately) into the visible world and "chained" (81d–e) to a new body, which can be an animal body suited to the character demonstrated in the previous life. Philosophy, on the other hand, is liberation from the prison of the body, and deliverance from sensual passions.

In the *Phaedo* passage the soul is considered to be a simple entity (a position congenial to Plotinus); in the *Republic* passage Plato is assuming the soul to be the composite tripartite (or at least composite) entity that he has described earlier in the work. Despite this composite nature the soul is immortal, having been "compounded in the finest way" (611b), and "related to the divine" (611e). But in our human condition in this life the soul's true nature is obscured, "associated as it is with the body and other evils" (611b), and with "the passions of human life" (612a). To understand its true nature, its "pure state" (611c), we must engage in philosophical reasoning. This section of the *Republic* uses the image of the sea god Glaukos to evoke the maimed and "encrusted" soul in this life: Plotinus cites this Plato text in lines 13–14 of the present chapter (see Commentary 12, 12–20). It is followed in the *Republic* by the myth of Er on afterlife judgments (see Commentary 11, 8–13).

What Plotinus is, in effect, proposing is an exploration of the apparently irreconcilable differences between Plato's position on afterlife judgments and his own views. His "argument" (*logos*, line 2) is opposed to the argument that he finds in Plato. A similar presentation of two opposing "arguments" on the soul's nature occurs in 2, 4 and 9 (see Commentary 2,

2–5), even if the issue there is of a quite different kind. Here he explores the differences on afterlife judgments against the background of the obvious agreement between him and Plato on the divine and immortal nature of the soul, on philosophy's purificatory role, on the risk of moral contamination by excessive preoccupation with things bodily, and on the reality of transmigration as a form of punishment.

12, 6–12 *For the argument granting faultlessness . . . not the other*: Plotinus recapitulates here his argument of Chapter 2 on the implications of a distinction between soul and its essence (see notes on 2, 1–13). The implication of what he says here is that Plato's view of the composite soul entails this distinction between soul and its essence. To elucidate the composite nature of soul he refers in line 9 to *Timaeus* 69c7–d1 (as in 8, 19–20: see Commentary 8, 18–23), asserting that "another form of soul" (*kai*, 9, emphasizes "another," hence my translation "quite another": see Denniston 319), the seat of the affections, is "woven into" the rational soul, making the whole soul ("affected in its entirety," 11) fallible and liable to punishment. This goes further than anything asserted by Plato in the *Republic* passage: Plotinus is drawing out the implications, in his view, of what Plato (*autō(i)*, 12, "for him," i.e. Plato) says there. By contrast, "the other" (*ekeino*, line 12) refers to the concept of the faultless, pure soul.

12, 12–20 *Hence he says . . . from everything that has been added*: With his reference to "the composite" (*suntheton*) in line 11 Plotinus has already cited *Republic* 611b5. He now goes on to quote a number of phrases, first, in lines 13–14, from *Republic* 611c7–d1, then in lines 14–17, scattered words and phrases from a longer section, *Republic* 611e1–612a4 (Szlezák 1979, 170–180, discusses echoes of this *Republic* passage in IV.7.10: see also Fleet 2016, 252–267). Plato in this text compares the soul in its pre-philosophical human state, "affected by many evils" (611d7), to the imagined appearance of the sea god Glaukos, partly damaged, encrusted with seashells and stones (one could imagine a statue of Glaukos that has been long in the water being like this). The soul has to have its accretions "chipped off" (611e5), so that its true nature, the potential of its "love of wisdom" (*philosophia*, 611e1), its immortality and kinship with the divine, may become apparent. In this passage Plato is talking about the possibility of purification in this life, even if he subsequently goes on to talk about afterlife rewards and punishments. Plotinus modifies Plato by extending the Glaukos simile to refer to the separation of the soul from body and from every "addition" at death. This becomes immediately clear in the following (lines 17–20). The "other life and other activities" must be those of the pure soul: Plotinus is repeating what he has said about the simple, non-composite soul in 2, 6–9. This pure soul is impeccable, and so cannot do anything for which it could be punished: what is punished must be "different" (line 18) from it. Plotinus does not say what this "different" entity is. We might expect that it must be the ensouled body, "illuminated" by the soul-trace, or the soul-trace itself, but this is not unproblematic: see lines 23–31.

In *Phaedo* 81b–c the unpurified soul is imagined departing to Hades tainted by the bodily element. We must allow for exaggerated metaphor here (and Plato qualifies the whole account of afterlife punishments by reiterated use of the word "probable" (*eikos*, 81d5–6, 81e2, 82a2, 82b5, etc.), or the phrase "as it is said" (81a8); see Hackforth 1955, 91), but this is the kind of assertion that leads Plotinus to say that, for Plato, the composite soul undergoes posthumous punishment (lines 10–12). And it is the case that the unpurified souls, and indeed the purified soul also (67c8, 83a7–8), are described using material metaphors in the *Phaedo* (Gallop 1975, 143–144). On the other hand, what Plato says about the pure soul in the *Phaedo* and *Republic* passages used here allows Plotinus to assert that soul's withdrawal and separation at death amount to total shedding of everything that has been added (lines 18–20, taking up the "what has been added" that he has inserted into the *Republic* quote in line 14), not just separation from the body. The following section of our chapter clarifies this: the philosophical soul will also shed the soul-trace.

12, 20–31 *For indeed the addition is at birth . . . if soul is wholly looking There*: Human birth entails the addition of the soul-trace, here unambiguously identified with "the other kind of soul" (line 21: again the phrase from *Timaeus* 69c7–d1, as in line 9). By "has been explained" (22) 7, 1–6 must be meant. HS refer to IV.8 [6], and that early treatise on the descent of soul elucidates the reference in the present chapter to the soul descending (*katabainousēs*, 22, cf. 27) and to its "decline" (*neusis*, 23 and 24, cf. 27), but it does not provide the precise account of the coming-into-being of the soul-trace and the living thing that Plotinus refers to here. Plotinus does, however, raise the question dealt with in IV.8, whether the soul's descent is a fault (*hamartia*, 24), and for that reason it is important to bear his argument there in mind when trying to understand our chapter (on IV.8 see Fleet 2012). In that treatise he is concerned to resolve apparent contradictions in Plato between the view (*Republic, Phaedrus*) that ascent is a liberation of the soul and its descent a "fall," and the positive view of the ensoulment of the universe in the *Timaeus* (IV.8.1). His solution is to see in ensoulment the positive ordering of matter *qua* spontaneous but necessary realization of a potential, namely the existence of the universe as manifestation and image of divine Intellect (IV.8.3–5). At the same time, the soul's "descent" entails activity at a level below that of Intellect, "in" which it remains, and, if the soul does not "look towards the intelligible" (IV.8.4, 14), its individualization, and turning away from Intellect (despite the fact that it is never separated from Intellect), and absorption with its life here, can become a "fault." In fact, Plotinus can speak of a double "fault" of the soul: on the one hand, its descent (for which the experience of descent is itself the "punishment"), and, on the other hand, its wrongdoing in its life here, which leads to reincarnation or other afterlife punishments (IV.8.5, 16–24). Souls become "amphibious," living in turn "the life There," in the intelligible, and the life here, and the quality of their lives determines the degree to which they are There or here (IV.8.4, 31–35). The motif of "wholly looking There" and "being wholly There" in the present chapter (lines 31 and 38) is an application of this passage in IV.8.4 to the problems under discussion here.

Plotinus' use of the term *neusis* ("decline") here and in V.1.10, 26–27 and III.6.5, 25 merely reinforces the theme of descent. He knows it as a Gnostic term (II.9.4, 6 and 11, 13), but it has no Gnostic connotations here or in the other cited passages (see Atkinson 1985, 225).

The present passage brings out clearly Plotinus' argument that the soul's "descent" is a manner of speaking ("it is said," line 27): in fact, the soul, as 7, 1–6 has insisted, does not descend, but a trace of it illuminates the body of the living thing. Here Plotinus provides another image of this: soul casts a shadow (26). Soul therefore is not at fault: Plotinus here is unequivocal, where the early IV.8.5, referred to above, speaks of descent as a fault of a kind. Here any responsibility is referred to the illuminated body (line 26), that is, the living thing.

The other question of the passage, whether the soul "abandons its image" (23–24, 28–29), namely in death (not stated explicitly, but that can be the only sense here), also seems to receive a clear answer, where earlier discussions were tentative or obscure. The "image" in question is the soul-trace (see 8, 17–18): Plotinus perhaps calls it the "image" (*eidōlon*) here in anticipation of the Homeric exegesis (where the *eidōlon/autos* distinction is made: see Commentary 12, 31–39) that follows. It can only exist if there is a body to receive it, and if the soul's "descent" generates it. Plotinus' phrase "if that which received it is not close by" (l. 29) uses the same metaphor of the "nearness" of body to soul-trace as in VI.4.15, 8–18, there in connection with the concept of the body's "aptitude" (*epitēdeiotēs*) to receive the soul-trace.

Unlike most translators, I have rendered the aorist participle as a past tense ("received,"line 29), as do HBT (Va, 297 with Vb, 449) and Marzolo 2006 (78: see Marzolo 174–179 for an extended discussion of the passage). Plotinus has used the past participle "has been illuminated" inline 28, as if imagining an embodiment of the soul-trace that has taken place: the past sequence is maintained in the following lines.

Now if the soul is "looking wholly There" (note that this is expressed as a condition), that is, totally turned towards the Intellect—something only possible, from the human perspective, for the philosopher, and here referring to state of the philosopher's soul at or after death—it is not generating any soul-trace: so "it <the image> is no longer there" (28–31). The full implications of this view become apparent only in the Herakles passage at the end of the chapter (see Commentary 12, 31–39). In the early IV.7 [2] Plotinus, starting from the Platonic assumption of a tripartite soul, asserts that, even if the "pure souls" (presumably the reasoning souls) are liberated from whatever has become attached to them at birth, namely the "worse part," this latter does not die, for it too is in virtue of its origin *qua* soul a part of real being (IV.7.14, 8–14: on IV.7 see Fleet 2016). In a difficult passage, VI.4.16, 36–48, the belief that souls go to Hades after death receives two explanations: souls are separated from their bodies, or they go to "some worse place." Plotinus talks of the "image" of the soul here, and this must either refer to the soul-trace that is familiar from our treatise (so Tornau), or to the lower, irrational soul (so Emilsson), the question of whose survival is discussed in IV.3.27–31 and IV.4.29 (see below). Plotinus seems to suggest in VI.4.16 either that that this image may remain with the soul, or, if philosophy has liberated the soul, the image may go "by itself to the worse place" (VI.4.16, 42–43). This latter can only mean some kind of new bodily incarnation. Its relevance to our chapter will become clearer in the Herakles section (see Commentary 12, 31–39). In IV.4.29 Plotinus is clearly reluctant to envisage annihilation of the lower soul at death: it may follow the soul's reason-principle, but, if not, it must continue somehow to exist. In the last part of the chapter, IV.4.29, 40–55, he concludes—anticipating the discussion of the present treatise—that the question needs further examination. Earlier in this long treatise he has argued, in a discussion of memory and the imagination, that the lower soul has its own posthumous memories (IV.3.27–31).

12, 31–39 *The poet seems . . . below as well*: Herakles is the last of the dead heroes in Hades encountered by Odysseus in the underworld book of the *Odyssey*. ". . . I saw mighty Herakles, / his image (*eidōlon*); but he himself (*autos*) among the immortal gods / enjoys their festivals and has as wife Hebe with the beautiful ankles, / child of great Zeus and Hera with golden sandals" (*Odyssey* XI 601–604). The passage is puzzling, for Herakles' double posthumous existence runs counter to the Homeric norm that, when one dies, one continues to exist as a bloodless *eidōlon* in Hades. The word *eidōlon* in Homer is often translated "shade" or "ghost," but is strictly speaking an exact "image" of the living person (Bremmer 1983, 78–82). Lines 602–604 have since antiquity often been considered a later interpolation (Heubeck 1989, 114 gives a balanced interpretation). But this does not concern Plotinus, and the passage is in some respects a godsend to him and, like Plutarch before him and other late readers of Homer, he can practise on it the kind of philosophical exegesis that Homer's authority attracted (on such exegesis in general see Lamberton 1989; on exegesis of the Herakles passage see Pépin 1971; Lamberton 1989, 102–103; on the present passage in the wider context of Plotinus' and other views see Kalligas 2014, 129–130). Plotinus refers to it in IV.3.27, 7–14 when arguing for the distinctive memories of the two souls, the rational "divine" soul and the lower soul when they are separated at death. It is also a subtext in VI.4.16, 36–47, of which more is said above and below. In the present chapter Plotinus attempts to do full justice to the two *logoi* ("versions," 33) of the passage. He will have noted that the deified Herakles among the gods is referred to as "himself" (*autos*), a term that for Plotinus can be equivalent to "the self" (see Commentary 10, 5–7; note the use of *autos* in connection with Herakles in IV.3.27, 13), the true Herakles—what, in *Alcibiades* 130c and *Laws* 959a–b the soul is. Herakles' virtues were practical ones, he was not a thinker (that is, a philosopher, *theōrētikos*, 37), he was not "wholly There" (38)—the precondition, as we have seen (31), for the liberation at death of the philosopher from all bodily existence—and so he is "above" as a deified hero, but at the same time "something of him" is below also, as an *eidōlon*. And that can surely only mean "in a body."

Plotinus presents this interpretation tentatively ("perhaps the story [*logos*] might be plausible," 35). It fits neatly with his developed theory of soul and soul-trace in this treatise, and it answers one question about the soul-trace's survival, if the dead person has not been a true philosopher—for we can assume that the exegesis applies not merely to the Homeric Herakles but to all humans. But it does not answer the question omitted by Plotinus here: in the case of the philosopher, in what sense is the soul-trace "no longer there"? In the other passages referred to above, Plotinus is clearly reluctant to envisage a total annihilation of the lower soul.

Perhaps here in one of his last treatises he goes so far as to posit the non-existence after death of what, after all, he has been arguing is a mere reflection of soul for the purpose of animating a particular body in a human life. Or perhaps the soul-trace is absorbed into the world-soul, existing, but potentially and not actually (as suggested by Tornau 1998, 318). But it is difficult to accept that the soul-trace, which Plotinus has stressed is a feature of the living thing and therefore embodied, can become part of soul, even in potential bodiless existence.

VI.4.16, 36–44 reflects on these same issues, but is difficult to interpret. There the reference to Hades as the invisible domain—echoing the etymology of *Phaedo* 80d5–7 as well as the doctrine of this Plato text (see Commentary 12, 1–5)—indicates that it is the desirable goal of the philosophically-liberated pure soul. But Plotinus offers an alternative interpretation of Hades as the "worse place" (VI.4.16, 38), that is, the traditional Greek concept of Hades as the dark underworld (where the Homeric Herakles' image is, in fact). The non-philosophical soul would presumably go there, and it would be some kind of bodily existence, with the image still being with the soul (or, as Plotinus puts it, with the soul being where the image is). But if philosophy has totally liberated the soul, "the image would then go to the worse place on its own" (VI.4.16, 41–43). "On its own (*monon*)" here can only mean "separately from the soul." But what kind of existence it would have in this state is unclear, and depends on the interpretation of "image" in this passage, alluded to above (see Commentary 12, 20–31): is it the soul-trace of our treatise (in which case the nature of its existence is puzzling, but must somehow be bodily), or is it the lower soul of IV.3.27 and other texts (in which case Plotinus is saying nothing new, and also not helping our understanding of I.1)?

On the question whether the lower soul is immortal see Blumenthal 1971, 94 with n. 21; see Smith 1974, 56–68, on Plotinus, Porphyry, and others.

Chapter 13

The final chapter returns to the question of the relation of the "we" to the human soul and to Intellect, asserts soul's non-bodily movement or alteration, and describes briefly how the soul is "intellectual."

13, 1–3 *That which has investigated . . . inasmuch as it is soul*: Plotinus' opening question returns to the table of contents of the first chapter, where (1, 9–11) it is said that the investigating subject should be considered. Who or what philosophizes, we or the soul? The answer foregrounds the "we," but Plotinus quickly rejects a mere instrumental role for the soul. The discursive reasoning soul, as often in Plotinus, is what "we" above all are (7, 14–17).

13, 3–5 *Will it be moved . . . but is its life*: Discursive reasoning can be described as a movement, from premisses to conclusions, from questions to answers, a kind of mental progression, as the practice of the present treatise has shown. Does the reasoning soul "move" then? Is there a non-bodily movement? It is important to remember that "movement" (*kinēsis*) can refer in Greek philosophical contexts to any kind of alteration. In III.6.3 Plotinus argues that living is not so much alteration of soul's nature, as actualization of a potential. When we say that soul is moved by desire or anger or opinions or reasoning, we mean that movements arise from soul, but that it remains the essentially the same (III.6.3, 22–35; see Aubry 338). Aristotle's influence is evident here. In *De Anima* I.4 Aristotle argues that to say the soul is in motion when we desire or perceive or think is misleading: ". . . saying that the soul is angry would be like saying that the soul weaves or builds . . . the human being does these things with the soul; and this is not insofar as there is motion in the soul, but rather because motion sometimes reaches as far as the soul, and sometimes proceeds from it" (408b11–16, trans. Shields). In *De Anima* II.5 the relation of motion to potentiality and actuality is developed, considering in particular the kind of alteration involved in perception (Fleet 1995, 113 discusses the influence of this passage on Plotinus). These Aristotle passages insulate Plotinus from too crude a view of the soul's movement, or of movement in the soul. It is not like bodily movement. But he cannot very well deny that soul moves, for that is Plato's view in the *Timaeus* and elsewhere, and Plotinus must somehow account for this. He attempts to do so in the early II.2 [14] in defence of Plato's concept in the *Timaeus* of the movement of universal soul, though here too he mentions movement in the human soul, which is not bodily, but (giving the examples of joy or attraction towards an apparent good) can be accompanied by bodily movement

(II.2.3, 12–15). There is a brilliant development in III.7.11–13 of the concept of time as "the life of the soul in a movement of passage from one way of life to another" (III.7.11, 43–45, trans. Armstrong; Pradeau 2010, 236 draws attention to II.2 and III.7 in the context of the present passage).

13, 5–8 *And intellection is ours . . . we shall ascend*: In Chapter 8 Plotinus has already explained in what way we "have" Intellect, even if it transcends the reasoning soul (8, 1–8). The soul is intellectual (*noera*) because, as the argument of V.1.3 explains, it comes from Intellect and can be considered as its matter, formed by Intellect as an independently existing being which is an expression or image of Intellect, an externalization of Intellect's activity. Intellect is the means of soul's perfection, when soul turns towards it and internalizes it *qua* object of thought (which entails being simultaneously one with Intellect *qua* thinking subject).

In V.3.3, 21–32 Plotinus has argued that we are not Intellect, in a passage where he presents the "we," perhaps more clearly than anywhere else in his treatises, as the reasoning soul. If in the present chapter he says that Intellect is "a part of us" (7–8), he is not necessarily contradicting that earlier argument (see Commentary 11, 4–8). When we "intelligize," exercising non-discursive thought, we are perforce one with Intellect, and, as IV.4.2 asserts, we take on unchangeability, and experience "unity" (*henōsis*) with Intellect, but without ceasing to be soul, for "both of them <soul and Intellect> are one and also two" (IV.4.2, 22–29).

Note that in our text Plotinus says that Intellect is "a part of us," not a part of soul (something he explicitly denies in V.3.3, 22–26). That is, he turns once again to the flexible concept of the "we" as focus of our consciousness at whatever level this consciousness operates. In V.3.4, 7–11 and 30, considering the "double" nature of self-knowledge, which can be the knowledge of the discursively reasoning soul or the intuitive knowledge of Intellect, he argues that the latter kind of self-knowledge is knowledge of oneself "no longer as a man," for "one has become Intellect." One transcends the level of discursive reason (here "man"), but the "we" is not transcended: rather, we "grasp" (*metalabontes*: see Ham 2000, 55 n. 41) Intellect, simultaneously knowing it and ourselves (V.3.4, 24–27).

When Plotinus says (lines 6–7) that intellection is a superior life, he is simply reiterating what he says elsewhere about the hierarchical order in which Intellect is superior to soul, and intellection is soul's perfect activity. In adding that Intellect acts towards us, he cannot mean that it inclines towards us (excluded in V.3.3, 43), but is referring to its activity as the productive sustaining cause of soul (V.1.7, 36–46; V.2.1, 13–18; see O'Meara 1993, 66).

The divine soul should "go up towards" towards divine Intellect (V 1, 3, 1–3; see Atkinson 1985, 46–70 on the themes of the chapter). This image of ascent is echoed in our passage's last words. Its Platonic credentials are clear: the ascent from the cave in the *Republic*, the fall and ascent themes of the *Phaedrus* myth, the ascent towards supreme Beauty in the *Symposium* (see Atkinson 1985, 47). Apart from the brief reference to the "god" (that is, the One or Good) in 8, 8–10, Plotinus does not comment on the ascent to that first principle in our treatise, but in the following final treatise in Porphyry's chronological list (I.7 [54] 1) he touches briefly on the theme of the soul's ultimate aspiration, its activity directed towards the Good. Note the future sense of the treatise's last word (*animen*: see LSJ, *aneimi*): this makes the soul's ascent here an eschatological one, something that the philosopher may look forward to as a permanent state after death, though "having Intellect" is also achievable momentarily in our temporal lives, as 8,1–8, 9,13–15, and 11, 4–8 have asserted, as well as IV.4.2 and V.3.3–4—cited above—and other texts, such as I.4.15, 21–25 and VI.5.7, 3–6 (cited with discussion in Commentary 10, 14–15 and 11, 4–8).

Select Bibliography

I. Ancient Authors

ALEXANDER OF APHRODISIAS: *De Anima Liber cum Mantissa*, ed. I. Bruns. Berlin: Reimer, 1887.

———: *De l'âme*, ed. M. Bergeron and R. Dufour. Greek Text (of Bruns), French Translation, Introduction, Commentary. Paris: Vrin, 2008.

———: *On the Soul*, Part I, V. Caston. Translation. London: Bloomsbury, 2012.

ARISTOTLE: *The Complete Works of Aristotle*, ed. J. Barnes. 2 vols. The Revised Oxford Translation. Princeton: Princeton University Press, 1984.

———: *De Anima*, ed. W. D.Ross. Greek Text, Introduction, Commentary. Oxford: Clarendon Press, 1961.

———: *De Anima*, C. Shields. Translation, Introduction, Commentary. Oxford: Clarendon Press, 2016.

———: *Metaphysics*, ed. W. D. Ross. Greek Text, Introduction, Commentary. 2 vols. Oxford: Clarendon Press, 1924.

———: *Metaphysics Z and H*, D. Bostock. Translation, Introduction, Commentary. Oxford: Clarendon Press, 1994.

———: *Posterior Analytics*, J. Barnes. Translation, Introduction, Commentary. 2nd edition. Oxford: Clarendon Press, 1993.

HOMER. *A Commentary on Homer's Odyssey*. Volume II, Books IX–XVI, ed. A. Heubeck and A. Hoekstra. Oxford: Clarendon Press, 1989.

NUMENIUS: *Fragments*, ed. É. des Places. Greek and Latin Text, French Translation, Notes. Paris: Les Belles Lettres, 1973.

PLATO: *Opera*, ed. J. Burnet. 5 vols. Clarendon Press: Oxford, 1900–1907.

———: *Opera*, ed. E. A. Duke et al. Vol. 1. Clarendon Press: Oxford, 1995.

———: *Complete Works*, ed. J. M. Cooper. Translation, Introduction, Notes. Indianapolis: Hackett, 1997.

———: *Alcibiades*, ed. N. Denyer. Greek Text, Introduction, Commentary. Cambridge: Cambridge University Press, 2001.

———: *Alcibiades*, ed. Ó. Velásquez. Greek Text, Introduction, Spanish Translation, Notes. Santiago de Chile: Ediciones Tacitas, 2013.

———: *Phaedo*, D. Gallop. Translation and Notes. Oxford: Clarendon Press, 1975.

———: *Phaedo*, R. Hackforth. Translation, Introduction, Commentary. Oxford: Clarendon Press, 1955.

———: *Phaedrus*, C. J. Rowe. Greek Text, Translation, Commentary. Warminster: Aris & Phillips, 1986.

———: *Philebus*, D. Frede. Translation, Introduction, Notes. Indianapolis: Hackett, 1993.

———: *Plato's Cosmology*, F. M. Cornford. Translation (of *Timaeus*) and Commentary. London: Routledge & Kegan Paul, 1937.

———: *Respublica*, ed. S. R. Slings. Clarendon Press: Oxford, 2003.

PORPHYRY: *Porphyrii Philosophi Fragmenta*, ed. A. Smith. Leipzig/Stuttgart: Teubner, 1993.

II. The *Enneads*: Editions, Translations, Commentaries

Armstrong, Arthur Hilary. 1966–1988. *Plotinus, Enneads*. Greek Text with English Translation and Introductions. 7 vols. Loeb Classical Library. Cambridge, Mass.: Harvard University Press. Revised edition of vol. I, 1989.

Atkinson, Michael J. 1985. *Plotinus: Ennead V.1, On the Three Principal Hypostases*. Oxford: Clarendon Press. Corrected reprint of the 1983 edition.

Beierwaltes, Werner. 1991. *Selbsterkenntnis und Erfahrung der Einheit. Plotins Enneade V 3.* Text, German translation, Commentary. Frankfurt am Main: Klostermann.

Bréhier, Émile. 1924–1938. *Plotin, Ennéades.* Greek Text and French Translation with Introductions and Notes. 7 vols. Paris: Les Belles Lettres.

Brisson, Luc and Pradeau, Jean-François (ed.). 2002–2010. *Plotin,Traités.* French Translation, Introductions, and Notes. 9 vols. Paris: Flammarion.

Dillon, John M. and Blumenthal, Henry J. 2015. *Plotinus. Ennead IV.3–IV.4.29. Problems Concerning the Soul.* Translation, Introduction, Commentary. Las Vegas, Zurich, Athens: Parmenides.

Emilsson, Eyjólfur K. and Strange, Steven, K. 2015. *Plotinus. Ennead VI.4 & VI.5. On the Presence of Being, One and the Same, Everywhere as a Whole.* Translation, Introduction, Commentary. Las Vegas, Zurich, Athens: Parmenides.

Fleet, Barrie. 1995. *Plotinus. Ennead III.6, On the Impassivity of the Bodiless.* Introduction, Greek Text, Translation, and Commentary. Oxford: Clarendon Press.

——— 2012. *Plotinus. Ennead IV.8. On the Descent of the Soul into Bodies*. Translation, Introduction, Commentary. Las Vegas, Zurich, Athens: Parmenides.

——— 2016. *Plotinus. Ennead IV.7. On the Immortality of the Soul*. Translation, Introduction, Commentary. Las Vegas, Zurich, Athens: Parmenides.

Gerson, Lloyd P. 2013. *Plotinus. Ennead V.5. That the Intelligibles are not External to the Intellect, and on the Good*. Translation, Introduction, Commentary. Las Vegas, Zurich, Athens: Parmenides.

Gurtler, Gary M. 2015. *Plotinus. Ennead IV.4.30–45 & IV.5. Problems Concerning the Soul*. Translation, Introduction, Commentary. Las Vegas, Zurich, Athens: Parmenides.

Hadot, Pierre. 1987. *Plotin: Traité 38 (VI, 7)*. Introduction, Translation, Commentary, and Notes. Paris: Cerf.

Ham, Bertrand. 2000. *Plotin: Traité 49 (V, 3)*. Introduction, Translation, Commentary, and Notes. Paris: Cerf.

Harder, Richard, Beutler, Rudolf, and Theiler, Willy. 1956–71. *Plotins Schriften*. Greek Text with German Translation and Commentary. 12 vols. Hamburg: Meiner.

Henry, Paul and Schwyzer, Hans-Rudolph. 1951–73. *Plotini Opera* I–III (editio maior). Paris: Desclée de Brouwer et Cie (HS_1).

——— 1964–1982. *Plotini Opera* I–III (editio minor, with revised text). Oxford: Clarendon Press (HS_2).

——— 1973. *Addenda et Corrigenda ad textum et apparatum lectionum.* In HS_1, t. III (HS_3).

——— 1982. *Addenda et Corrigenda ad textum et apparatum lectionum.* In HS_2, t. III (HS_4).

Kalligas, Paul. 2014. *The Enneads of Plotinus: A Commentary.* Volume 1. Translated by E. K. Fowden and N. Pilavachi. Princeton and Oxford: Princeton University Press.

McGroarty, Kieran. 2006. *Plotinus on* Eudaimonia*: A Commentary on Ennead I.4.* Introduction, Greek Text, Translation, and Commentary. Oxford: Oxford University Press.

MacKenna, Stephen. 1962[3]. *Plotinus: The Enneads.* English Translation Revised by B. S. Page. London: Faber & Faber.

——— 1991. *Plotinus: The Enneads.* Selected Treatises Revised with Notes by John Dillon. London: Penguin.

Meijer, P. A. 1992. *Plotinus on the Good or the One (Enneads VI, 9): An Analytical Commentary.* Amsterdam: Gieben and Leiden: Brill.

O'Meara, Dominic. 1999. *Plotin: Traite 51 (I, 8).* Introduction, Translation, Commentary, and Notes. Paris: Cerf.

Schwyzer, Hans-Rudolph. 1987. "Corrigenda ad Plotini Textum." *Museum Helveticum* 44, 181–210 (HS_5).

Tornau, Christian. 1998. *Plotin, Enneaden VI 4–5 [22–23]: Ein Kommentar.* Stuttgart/Leipzig: Teubner.

Wilberding, James. 2006. *Plotinus' Cosmology: A Study of Ennead II.1 (40).* Text, Translation, and Commentary. Oxford: Oxford University Press.

III. Studies on *Ennead* I.1 and Related Works

Aubry, Gwenaëlle. 2004. *Plotin: Traité 53 (I, 1).* Introduction, Translation, Commentary, and Notes. Paris: Cerf.

Blumenthal, Henry J. 1971. *Plotinus' Psychology: His Doctrines of the Embodied Soul.* The Hague: Nijhoff.

Caluori, Damian. 2015. *Plotinus on the Soul.* Cambridge: Cambridge University Press.

Dörrie, Heinrich. 1957. "Kontroversen um die Seelenwanderung im kaiserzeitlichen Platonismus," *Hermes* 85, 414–435.

Emilsson, Eyjólfur K. 1988. *Plotinus on Sense-Perception: A Philosophical Study.* Cambridge: Cambridge University Press.

Gurtler, Gary M. 1988. *Plotinus: The Experience of Unity.* New York/Bern: Peter Lang.

——— 2005. "Plotinus: Self and Consciousness," in *History of Platonism: Plato Redivivus*, ed. J. F. Finamore and R. M. Berchman. New Orleans: University Press of the South, 113–129.

Marzolo, Carlo. 2006. *Plotino, Che cos'è l'essere vivente e che cos'è l'uomo? (I 1 [53])*. Introduction, Greek Text, Translation and Commentary. Preface by C. D'Ancona. Pisa: Pisa University Press.

Morelli, Eric J. 2011. "Plotinus' Two Interpretations of *Timaeus* 35a," *Ancient Philosophy* 31, 351–361.

O'Daly, Gerard J. P. 1973. *Plotinus' Philosophy of the Self.* Shannon: Irish University Press (reprinted in O'Daly 2001, Study I).

——— 2001. *Platonism Pagan and Christian: Studies in Plotinus and Augustine*. Aldershot: Ashgate/Variorum.

Pépin, Jean. 1971. "Héraclès et son reflet dans le néoplatonisme," in *Le Néoplatonisme*. Colloques Royaumont, 9–13 juin 1969. Paris: Éditions du CNRS, 167–192.

Pradeau, Jean-François. 2010. *Plotin, Traité 53 (I, 1).Qu'est que le vivant?* Introduction, Translation, and Notes. In *Plotin, Traités 51–54. Porphyre, Vie de Plotin*, ed. L. Brisson and J.-F. Pradeau. Paris: Flammarion, 169–236.

Remes, Pauliina. 2007. *Plotinus on Self: The Philosophy of the 'We'*. Cambridge: Cambridge University Press.

Rich, A. N. M. 1957. "Reincarnation in Plotinus," *Mnemosyne*, ser. 4.10, 232–238.

Schroeder, Frederic. M. 1987. "Synousia, Synaisthesis and Synesis. Presence and Dependence in the Plotinian Philosophy of Consciousness," in *Aufstieg und Niedergang der römischen Welt*, ed. H. Temporini and W. Haase. Vol. II, 36, 1. Berlin/New York: de Gruyter, 677–699.

Schwyzer, Hans-Rudolf. 1960. "«Bewusst» und «Unbewusst» bei Plotin," in *Les sources de Plotin*. Entretiens sur l'antiquité classique, 5. Vandœuvres/Geneva: Fondation Hardt, 341–378 (discussion 379–390).

Sorabji, Richard. 2006. *Self: Ancient and Modern Insights about Individuality, Life, and Death*. Oxford: Clarendon Press.

Stamatellos, Giannis. 2013. "Plotinus on Transmigration: A Reconsideration," *Journal of Ancient Philosophy* 7, 49–64.

Stern-Gillet, Suzanne. 2007. "Consciousness and Introspection in Plotinus and Augustine," in *Proceedings of the Boston Area Colloquium in Ancient Philosophy*, ed. J. J. Cleary and G. M. Gurtler, 145–173.

Tornau, Christian. 2009. "Qu'est-ce qu'un individu? Unité, individualité et conscience de soi dans la métaphysique plotinienne de l'âme," *Les études philosophiques* 90/3, 333–360.

——— 2011. *Plotin: Ausgewählte Schriften.* Translation and Commentary. Stuttgart: Reclam [I.1: 311–324, 424–431].

Warren, E. W. 1964. "Consciousness in Plotinus," *Phronesis* 9, 83–97.

IV. General Publications

Ackrill, John L. 1981. *Aristotle the Philosopher.* Oxford: Oxford University Press.

——— 1997."Aristotle's Definitions of *Psuchē*," in Id., *Essays on Plato and Aristotle.* Oxford: Oxford University Press, 163–178 (first published in *Proceedings of the Aristotelian Society*, 73, 1973).

Blumenthal, Henry J. 1976. "Plotinus' Adaptation of Aristotle's Psychology: Sensation, Imagination and Memory," in *The Significance of Neoplatonism*, ed. R. Baine Harris. Norfolk, Va.: Old Dominion University, 41–58.

——— 1996. *Aristotle and Neoplatonism in Late Antiquity: Interpretations of De Anima.* Ithaca, NY: Cornell University Press.

Bremmer, Jan. 1983. *The Early Greek Concept of the Soul.* Princeton: Princeton University Press.

Clark, Stephen R. L. 2016. *Plotinus: Myth, Metaphor, and Philosophical Practice.* Chicago and London: University of Chicago Press.

Cooper, John M. 1980. "Aristotle on Friendship," in *Essays on Aristotle's Ethics,* ed. A. O. Rorty. Berkeley/Los Angeles: University of California Press, 301–340.

Corrigan, Kevin. 2005. *Reading Plotinus: A Practical Introduction to Neoplatonism.* West Lafayette, Ind.: Purdue University Press.

——— 1996. *Plotinus' Theory of Matter-Evil and the Question of Substance: Plato, Aristotle, and Alexander of Aphrodisias.* Leuven: Peeters.

Dillon, John M. 1977/1996$_2$. *The Middle Platonists: A Study of Platonism, 80 B.C. to A.D. 220.* London: Duckworth.

——— 1983. "Plotinus, Philo and Origen on the Grades of Virtue," in *Platonismus und Christentum. Festschrift für Heinrich Dörrie,* ed. H.-D. Blume and F. Mann. Münster: Aschendorff, 92–105.

———. 2013. "Plotinus and the Vehicle of the Soul," in *Gnosticism, Platonism and the Late Antique World: Essays in Honor of John D. Turner,* ed. K. Corrigan and T. Rasimus. Leiden: Brill, 485–496.

Dodds, Eric R. 1973. "Tradition and Personal Achievement in the Philosophy of Plotinus," in Id., *The Ancient Concept of Progress and other Essays on Greek*

Literature and Belief. Oxford: Clarendon Press, 126–139 (first published in the *Journal of Roman Studies* 50, 1960).

Dover, Kenneth J. 1974. *Greek Popular Morality in the Time of Plato and Aristotle.* Oxford: Basil Blackwell.

Emilsson, Eyjólfur K. 2007. *Plotinus on Intellect.* Oxford: Clarendon Press.

——— 2017. *Plotinus.* London and New York: Routledge.

Ferwerda, Rein. 1965. *La signification des images et des métaphores dans la pensée de Plotin.* Groningen: Wolters.

——— 1984. "Pity in the Life and Thought of Plotinus," in D. T. Runia (ed.), *Plotinus amid Gnostics and Christians.* Amsterdam: Free University Press, 53–72.

Festugière, André-Jean. 1969. "L'ordre de lecture des dialogues de Platon aux Ve/VIe siècles," *Museum Helveticum* 26, 281–296.

Gerson, Lloyd P. 1994. *Plotinus.* London: Routledge.

——— ed. 1996. *The Cambridge Companion to Plotinus.* Cambridge: Cambridge University Press.

——— ed. 2010. *The Cambridge History of Philosophy in Late Antiquity.* 2 vols. Cambridge: Cambridge University Press.

Grafton, Anthony and Williams, Megan. 2006. *Christianity and the Transformation of the Book: Origen, Eusebius, and the Library of Caesarea*. Cambridge, MA: Harvard University Press.

Henry, Paul. 1960. "Une comparaison chez Aristote, Alexandre et Plotin," in *Les sources de Plotin*. Entretiens sur l'antiquité classique, 5. Vandœuvres/Geneva: Fondation Hardt, 427–444 (discussion 445–449).

Igal, Jesús. 1979. "Aristóteles y la evolución de la antropología de Plotino," *Pensiamento* 35, 315–345.

Lamberton, Robert. 1989. *Homer the Theologian: Neoplatonist Allegorical Reading and the Growth of the Epic Tradition*. Berkeley/Los Angeles: University of California Press.

Lee, J. Scott. 1979. "The Doctrine of Reception According to the Capacity of the Recipient in *Ennead* VI.4–5," *Dionysius* 3, 79–97.

Noble, Christopher I. 2013. "How Plotinus' Soul Animates his Body: The Argument for the Soul-Trace at *Ennead* IV.4.18.1–9," *Phronesis* 58, 249–279.

O'Meara, Dominic J. 1980. "The Problem of Omnipresence in Plotinus, *Ennead* VI, 4–5: A Reply," *Dionysius* 4, 61–73.

——— 1993. *Plotinus: An Introduction to the Enneads.* Oxford: Clarendon Press.

Remes, Pauliina, 2008. *Neoplatonism.* Berkeley/Los Angeles: University of California Press.

Renaud, François and Tarrant, Harold. 2015. *The Platonic Alcibiades I: The Dialogue and its Ancient Reception.* Cambridge: Cambridge University Press.

Rist, John M. 1967. *Plotinus: The Road to Reality.* Cambridge: Cambridge University Press.

——— 1962. "Theos and the One in some Texts of Plotinus," *Mediaeval Studies* 24, 169–180.

Rutherford, Richard B. 1995. *The Art of Plato: Ten Essays in Platonic Interpretation.* London: Duckworth.

Sandbach, F. H. 1975. *The Stoics.* London: Chatto & Windus.

Schniewind, Alexandrine. 2003. *L'Éthique du Sage chez Plotin.* Paris: J. Vrin.

Sharples, Robert W. 1996. *Stoics, Epicureans and Sceptics: An Introduction to Hellenistic Philosophy.* London and NewYork: Routledge.

Slaveva-Griffin, Svetla. 2009. *Plotinus on Number.* Oxford: Oxford University Press.

Szlezák, Thomas A. 1979. *Platon und Aristoteles in der Nuslehre Plotins.* Basel/Stuttgart: Schwabe.

Smith, Andrew 1974. *Porphyry's Place in the Neoplatonic Tradition: A Study in Post-Plotinian Neoplatonism.* The Hague: Nijhoff.

——— 2004. *Philosophy in Late Antiquity.* London and New York: Routledge.

——— 2006. "The Object of Perception in Plotinus," in *Eriugena, Berkeley, and the Idealist Tradition,* ed. S. Gersh and D. Moran. Notre Dame, Ind.: University of Notre Dame Press, 95–104.

Wallis, Richard T. 1972/1995$_2$. *Neoplatonism.* London: Duckworth.

Index of Ancient Authors

Albinus

Eisagōgē
149, 35–36 20

Alexander of Aphrodisias

On the Soul
12, 7–19 67
14, 4–5, 17–19 91
15, 9–29 91
20, 26–21, 21 92

Anaxagoras
fr. B 1 57, 127–128

Aristotle

De Anima (On the Soul)
I.1, 402a7–10 136
I.1, 403a3–5 139
I.1, 403a10–12 69
I.1, 403a16–b19 109–110
I.1, 407b13–26 117
I.3, 407b20–26 85
I.3, 407b25–26 93
I.4, 408b11–15 103
I.4, 408b11–16 181
I.4, 408b12–13 52
II.1, 408b28–29 53, 105
II.1, 412a16–17 53, 105
II.1, 412a16–21 118
II.1, 412a19–20 74
II.1, 412a27–b1 52, 102
II.1, 412b6 101–102
II.1, 412b11–15 101
II.1, 412b27–28 101
II.1, 413a6–7 94
II.1, 413a8–9 91
II.4, 415b15–20 86
II.5 181
II.6, 418a16–20 138

II.12, 424a17–24 81
III.1, 425a14–b3 138
III.8, 432a2 129
III.10, 433b16–18 106

Eudemian Ethics
VII.9, 1241b17–24 85

On Generation and Corruption
I.7, 323b23–27 99

Metaphysics
VII.6, 1031a15–b1448, 62, 73–74
VIII.3, 1043a29–b448, 62, 73

Nicomachean Ethics
II.5, 1105b21–23 67
II.5,1105b23 149
II.7, 1107a33–b4 67
III.1, 1109b31–32 149
III.1, 1110b28–1111a2 149

Homer
Odyssey XI 601–60463, 176

Numenius
fr. 2, 16 57, 129

Parmenides
fr. 8, 5 128

Plato

Alcibiades
129b–130b 68
129c–e 85
129d 86
130a9 68, 105, 106
130c 144, 177

Laws
959a–b 177

Phaedo
66b–c 87
66b–d 98
66d6 143
67a2–4 94–95
67c–d 147
67c5–d10 89
66d1–2 87
80c–84b 167
81b–c 171
82a11–b3 148

Phaedrus
229e 21
235b–c 161
246b6 134
246c5 50, 65, 85, 123
248a–b 143

Philebus
50e–55c 82

Republic
518e1–2 60, 148
588c–590b 124, 142
588c7 56, 124, 145
588d3 56, 124

589a7–b160, 123, 142, 150
590a9–b1 56, 124
611b–612a 167–168
611b5 62
611c7–d1 62, 170
611d7 170
611e1–612a4 62, 170
614b 161

Symposium
209b7 105

Theaetetus
198d 139

Timaeus
35a1–4 57, 130–131
36e50, 52, 90, 100, 155–156
43b6 143
44a–c 155
69c7–d158, 133, 169, 171
87e5–6 105

PLOTINUS

Enneads
I.2.2, 14–17 148
I.2.3, 15–19 147
I.2.6, 4–6 146
I.4.9–10 140
I.4.10, 10–16 160
I.4.15, 21–25 150, 184
I.7.1 184
II.2.3, 12–15 181–182
II.3.9, 30–31 145
II.3.16, 1–4 18, 27, 80
II.9.2, 4–6 153
II.9.17, 52 155
III.1.7, 15–20 155
III.4.2, 1–15 134
III.4.2, 25–28 162
III.6.1, 1–7 70
III.6.1, 36–37 163
III.6.2–4 87–88
III.6.2, 39–44 163
III.6.3, 22–35 181
III.6.5, 1–2, 19 89–90
III.6.5, 25 173
III.6.7, 23–26 132
III.6.9, 12–13 99–100
III.6.13, 34–55 132
III.7.11, 43–45 182
IV.2.2, 49–55 131
IV.3.4, 23, 25 134
IV.3.4, 31–33 87
IV.3.4, 36–37 87
IV.3.6, 10–15 118
IV.3.10, 38–40 117
IV.3.12, 1–12 132
IV.3.12, 11–12 134
IV.3.21, 11–19 92
IV.3.22 100
IV.3.22, 3 163
IV.3.25, 38–42 85
IV.3.27–31 175

IV.3.27, 7–14 176–177
IV.3.27, 13 177
IV.3.30 159–160
IV.3.31, 15 146
IV.4.2, 22–29 182
IV.4.18, 2–4 164
IV.4.18, 6–7 117
IV.4.20–21 118
IV.4.23 121–122
IV.4.23, 15–19 120
IV.4.23, 21–22 142
IV.4.28, 52–55 117
IV.4.29, 40–55 175
IV.4.29, 50–51 117
IV.5.1, 1–13 120
IV.6.1, 14–40 120
IV.6.3, 19–25 155
IV.7.1, 24–25 146
IV.7.8², 20–22 98
IV.7.9, 26–29 98–99
IV.7.10 170
IV.7.14, 1–5 164
IV.7.14, 1–8 162
IV.7.14, 8–14 174–175
IV.8 172–173
IV.8.4, 18–21 87
IV.8.4, 31–35 95, 173
IV.8.8, 1–6 117
IV.8.8, 5–7 159
IV.9.3, 1–4 151
IV.9.3, 23–28 118
V.1.3, 1–4 130, 183
V.1.7, 36–46 183
V.1.10, 24–31 95
V.1.10, 26–27 173
V.1.12, 5–12 159
V.1.12, 5–21 125
V.1.12, 18–19 95
V.1.12, 20–21 159
V.2.1, 13–18 183
V.3.3, 21–32 182–183
V.3.3, 27–29 158
V.3.3, 31–32 157
V.3.3, 35–40 154
V.3.3, 43 183
V.3.3, 45 – 4,4 157–158
V.3.4, 7–11 183
V.3.4, 13 127
V.3.4, 24–27 183
V.3.4, 30 183
V.3.9, 1 127
V.5.1 126
V.8.11, 31–34 157
V.9.6, 15–20 117
VI.2.5, 19–26 75–76
VI.4.1, 2–3 131
VI.4.3, 19–23 117
VI.4.4, 32–33 131
VI.4.15, 1–8 118
VI.4.15, 8–18 117, 174
VI.4.16, 4–5 161
VI.4.16, 6–7 162

VI.4.16, 36–37 167
VI.4.16, 36–48 175, 177–179
VI.5.7, 3–6 157, 184
VI.7.5, 21–25 129
VI.7.6, 21–23 162
VI.7.7, 1–5 162
VI.7.7, 8–17 118
VI.7.14, 18–23 151
VI.7.17, 34–36 129
VI.7.41, 22–25 19
VI.8.14, 4–7 78–79

PORPHYRY

Vita Plotini (Life of Plotinus)
6, 16–25 17
6, 22 65
6, 34–37 17
24, 15–16 18
24, 16–17 18
24, 18 65

STOICORUM VETERUM FRAGMENTA
II 473 105–106
III 378 67
III 394 149

Index of Names and Subjects

Ackrill, J. L. 73, 102
affections 47–48, 50–55, 59, 67–71, 81–82, 87–89, 98, 102, 105, 108–110, 117, 139–140, 145
afterlife punishments 61–63, 160–164, 166–169
Albinus 20
Alcinous 118
Alexander of Aphrodisias 21–22, 27, 91–92, 98, 118
Anaxagoras 127–128
anger 109–110
animals 61, 160–165
apprehension, *see* consciousness
Aristotle
- influence of *De Anima* on Plotinus 27, 85–86, 90–91, 102–103, 117–118, 181
- on affections 69
- on kinds of separation 89
- on the Delphic precept 21
- "soul"/"to be soul" distinction 48, 62, 72–77, 169

Armstrong, A. H. 123, 141, 143
Atkinson, M. J. 159, 173, 183, 184
Aubry, G. 69, 78, 82, 87, 90, 98, 107, 113, 127, 130, 141, 152, 160, 164, 181

Barnes, J. 76
Beierwaltes, W. 154
Beutler, R. 150
Blumenthal, H. J. 23n, 24n, 26n, 27n, 92, 93, 100, 117, 118, 120–122, 124, 129, 131, 132, 133, 142, 163, 179
body-soul relation 18–19, 117–119, 130–133
  "animal" 60, 145
  axe analogy 52, 101–102
  capacity of recipient body 163
  combination (*sunamphoteron*) 53, 55, 85, 101, 105, 107, 136
  common entity (*koinon*) 53, 58, 59, 60, 105, 136, 142–143
  commonality 55–56, 59, 118, 139–140
  composite (*suntheton*) 60, 153, 169–170
  in Plato 68–69, 130–131, 133–134
  instrumentalism 50–52, 89, 103
    craftsman-tool analogy 50, 85–86
    helmsman-ship analogy 51, 91–93
  light analogy 52, 55, 56, 100, 117, 132, 164
  living thing 24, 28, 50, 52, 53, 55, 61, 65, 85, 103, 160, 162–163
  mixed/unmixed 18, 28, 47, 49, 50–51, 69–70, 80, 90–96, 97–100
  mirror-image 58, 132–133
  mirror of Dionysos 132
  qualified body 55, 105, 117–118
  transmission 107
book-roll 128–129
Bostock, D. 73
Bremmer, J. 176

Caluori, D. 23n, 118, 164
children 60, 152–156
Cicero 21
Clark, S. R. L. 133
common perception (*koinē aisthēsis*) 59, 137–138
consciousness 25, 59, 61, 139–141, 156, 158–160, 162–163, 183
conversion 58, 153
Cooper, J. M. 150
Corrigan, K. 76
Courcelle, P. 19n, 21n

death 60, 147–148, 166–179
Delphic precept ("Know Thyself") 19–22, 69
Denyer, N. 20n, 69
desire 49, 51, 53, 106, 110
Dillon, J. M. 23n, 26n, 92, 100, 118, 121–122, 131, 132, 147, 163
Dodds, E. R. 115, 140
Dörrie, H. 161
Dover, K. J. 21n, 149, 150

Emilsson, E. K. 23n, 24n, 118, 120–121, 128, 130, 131, 137, 141, 142, 157, 163, 164, 175
Empedocles 151, 161
essence, essential, *see* substance, substantial
evil 53, 58, 108–109, 135–137

Ferwerda, R. 133, 149
Festugière, A.-J. 20n
Fleet, B. 23n, 68, 88, 98, 100, 132, 162, 164, 170, 172, 175, 181

Forms (*see also* soul as form) 24, 56, 57, 59, 121, 127–129, 140, 141
friendship/love 60, 150–151

Gerson, L. P. 126
"God" 57, 129, 184
Good, *see* One
Gollwitzer, T. 81
Glaukos 62, 168, 170
Gurtler, G. M. 23n, 131, 140, 142

Hackforth, R. 171
Hades 61, 63, 175–179
Hadot, P. 130
Ham, B. 154, 158, 183
Henry, P. 146
Herakles 63, 174–177
Heubeck, A. 176
Homer 63, 176–179
hypostases 27, 79

Igal, J. 27n, 140
impressions (*tupoi*) 56, 120, 140
Intellect (*nous*) 24, 25, 57, 59, 60, 61, 64, 122–123, 126–129, 138–139, 150, 153–159, 182–183
intellection (*noēsis*) 48, 49, 64, 70–71, 82, 141
intelligibles (*noēta*) 56, 59, 120–121

judgments after death 61, 166

Kalligas, P. 162, 176

Lamberton, R. 176
Lee, J. S. 118, 163
living thing (*zō(i)on*) *see under* body-soul relation

McGroarty, K. 140, 151
man (*anthrōpos*) 54, 65, 111, 183
    "true/inner man" 56, 60, 123–124, 146, 150
Marzolo, C. 67, 94, 106, 110, 117, 174
Meijer, P. A. 129
memory 132, 146, 155, 164, 175
Morelli, E. J. 131

Noble, C. I. 118

O'Daly, G. 19n, 25n, 145
O'Meara, D. J. 118, 149, 183
One (Good) 27, 54, 110, 129–130, 153, 184
opinion 47, 53–54, 58, 70, 82, 88, 121, 136

Parmenides 128
passions, *see* affections
Pausanias 19n
Pépin, J. 176
perception (*aisthēsis*) 24, 28–29, 48–51, 53, 55–56, 58–59, 71, 81–82, 86–89, 98, 114–115, 119–122, 133, 137, 139–142, 155, 159
philosophy, philosophizing 50, 62, 63, 70–71, 89, 94, 148–149, 170, 177, 180
pity 149
pleasure 49, 51, 82

Plato
  Alcibiades 20–21, 68–69, 144
  on afterlife judgments 166–169
  on composition of world-soul 130–131
  on human soul 26, 68–69, 76–77, 85, 57, 89–90, 93, 98, 123–125, 155, 166–168, 170–171
  on transmigration 160–162
  soul "woven through" universe 50, 52, 90, 100
  use of myths 160–161
Plotinus
  argument and method in I.1 22
  style in I.1 28, 79
Porphyry 17, 22, 65
  as editor of Plotinus 18–19, 65
Pradeau, J.-F. 67, 143, 182
purification 146–147, 167, 170, 171
Pythagoras 161

Remes, P. 25n, 145
Renaud, F. 20n, 69
representation/imagination (*phantasia*) 58, 137, 160
responsibility 58, 135–136
Rich, A. N. M. 162
Ross, W. D. 73
Rutherford, R. B. 161

Sandbach, F. H. 149
Schroeder, F. M. 140
Schwyzer, H.-R. 140
self ("we") 19, 24–26, 111, 143
  "amphibious" 95, 173

and consciousness 124–125, 156–160, 183
and Intellect 57, 138–139, 156–160, 182–184
and perception 119, 122–123
and soul 59–60, 63–64, 130, 158, 180–182
and the One 57, 184
autos referring to self 145–146, 177
"double" 25, 60, 145–146, 156
"multiple" 25, 136–137, 156
"we"/"ours" distinction 25, 56, 59–60, 63–64, 122–123, 127–128, 139, 158, 182–183
sensation 24, 56, 59, 71, 120–122, 137, 140–141, 163–164
sex 54, 80, 111
Sharples, R. W. 151
Shields, C. 86, 89, 91, 138, 139
Sleeman, J. H. 94
Smith, A. 179
Sorabji, R. 25n
soul (*see also* transmigration of souls)
and individual identity 26
ascent of 183–184
as form 78, 100–102
"care for the body" 50, 86–87, 134
conversion of 95, 134, 153–154, 174
"decline" of 62, 173
"descent" of 23, 62, 132, 172–173
"divisible" in bodies 131–133
fault/faultless 61, 62, 169, 170, 172–173
image (*eidōlon*) 61–63, 173–174, 176–178
immortality 26, 48
impassive 48, 52, 53, 78–79, 102, 144–145, 163–164
indivisible 127

"movement" of soul 63–64, 87–88, 103, 180–182
not composite/simple 49, 61–62, 78–79, 170
"on its own" 82–83
"parts"/faculties/powers of soul 53–54, 58, 62, 93–94, 109, 112–114, 122–125, 133–134, 153–154
reason, reasoning soul 57, 58–60, 70, 82, 122–125, 126–128, 141–142, 144–145, 148–149, 154–155, 158
relation to Intellect 27
separation from body 50–51, 60, 61, 62, 89–90, 94–95, 147
souls of animals 160–165
soul-trace 23–25, 62–63, 117, 142, 147–148, 170–179
soul-vehicle 122
"the middle" 61, 154–155
unchanging 142, 144
undescended into body 23, 117, 141, 153
use of "soul"/"to be soul" distinction 48, 62, 75–78, 169
world-soul 23–24, 61, 118, 133, 164, 178
"woven through" universe 50, 52, 90, 100
Stamatellos, G. 162
Stern-Gillet, S. 26n
Stoics on soul-body blending/mixture 69–70, 90, 97–99, 105–106
Strange, S. K.118, 131, 163
substance, substantial 49, 57, 80–81, 118–119
sympathy 141–142
Szlezák, T. A. 123, 170

Tarrant, H. 20n, 69
Theiler, W. 96, 108–109, 113

Tornau, C. 25n, 80, 108–109, 110, 111, 114, 118, 123, 128, 131, 137, 143, 156, 159, 175, 178
"There" 63, 173–174, 177
transmigration of souls 160–164

undiminished giving 79

Velásquez, Ó. 20n, 69
vices 149
virtues 60, 63, 146–148, 177

Warren, E. W.
"we", *see* self
Wilberding, J. 124

Xenophon 21

• ALSO AVAILABLE FROM PARMENIDES PUBLISHING •

PRE-SOCRATICS

By Being, It Is: *The Thesis of Parmenides* by Néstor-Luis Cordero

The Fragments of *Parmenides*: *A Critical Text with Introduction and Translation, the Ancient Testimonia and a Commentary by A. H. Coxon. Revised and Expanded Edition edited with new Translations by Richard McKirahan and a new Preface* by Malcolm Schofield

The Legacy of Parmenides: *Eleatic Monism and Later Presocratic Thought* by Patricia Curd

Parmenides and the History of Dialectic: *Three Essays* by Scott Austin

Parmenides, Venerable and Awesome: *Proceedings of the International Symposium* edited by Néstor-Luis Cordero

Presocratics and Plato: *A Festschrift in Honor of Charles Kahn* edited by Richard Patterson, Vassilis Karasmanis, and Arnold Hermann

The Route of Parmenides: *Revised and Expanded Edition, With a New Introduction, Three Supplemental Essays, and an Essay* by Gregory Vlastos by Alexander P. D. Mourelatos

To Think Like God: *Pythagoras and Parmenides. The Origins of Philosophy. Scholarly and fully annotated edition* by Arnold Hermann

The Illustrated To Think Like God: P*ythagoras and Parmenides. The Origins of Philosophy* by Arnold Hermann (with over 200 full color illustrations)

PLATO

A Stranger's Knowledge: *Statesmanship, Philosophy, and Law in Plato's Statesman* by Xavier Márquez

God and Forms in Plato by Richard D. Mohr

Image and Paradigm in Plato's Sophist by David Ambuel

Imperial Plato: Albinus, Maximus, Apuleius by Ryan Fowler

Interpreting Plato's Dialogues by J. Angelo Corlett

One Book, the Whole Universe: *Plato's Timaeus Today* edited by Richard D. Mohr and Barbara M. Sattler

Platonic Patterns: *A Collection of Studies* by Holger Thesleff

Plato's Late Ontology: *A Riddle Resolved* by Kenneth M. Sayre

Plato's Parmenides: *Text, Translation & Introductory Essay* by Arnold Hermann. Translation in collaboration with Sylvana Chrysakopoulou with a Foreword by Douglas Hedley

Plato's Universe by Gregory Vlastos

The Philosopher in Plato's Statesman by Mitchell Miller

ARISTOTLE

Aristotle's Empiricism: Experience and Mechanics in the Fourth Century B.C. by Jean De Groot

One and Many in Aristotle's Metaphysics—*Volume I: Books Alpha-Delta* by Edward C. Halper

One and Many in Aristotle's Metaphysics—*Volume 2: The Central Books* by Edward C. Halper

Reading Aristotle: Physics VII.3 "What is Alteration?" *Proceedings of the International ESAP-HYELE Conference* edited by Stefano Maso, Carlo Natali, and Gerhard Seel

HELLENISTIC PHILOSOPHY

A Life Worthy of the Gods: *The Materialist Psychology of Epicurus* by David Konstan

THE *ENNEADS* OF PLOTINUS

Translations with Introductions & Philosophical Commentaries
Series edited by John M. Dillon and Andrew Smith

Ennead **I.6:** ***On Beauty*** by Andrew Smith

Ennead **II.5:** ***On What Is Potentially and What Actually*** by Cinzia Arruzza

Ennead **II.9:** ***Against the Gnostics*** by Sebastian Ramon Philipp Gertz

Ennead **IV.3–IV.4.29:** ***Problems concerning the Soul*** by John M. Dillon and H. J. Blumenthal

Ennead **IV.4.30–45 & IV.5:** ***Problems concerning the Soul*** by Gary M. Gurtler

Ennead IV.7: ***On the Immortality of the Soul*** by Barrie Fleet

Ennead **IV.8:** ***On the Descent of the Soul into Bodies*** by Barrie Fleet

Ennead **V.1:** ***On the Three Primary Levels of Reality*** by Eric D. Perl

Ennead **V.5:** ***That the Intelligibles are not External to the Intellect, and on the Good*** by Lloyd P. Gerson

Ennead **VI.4 & VI.5:** ***On the Presence of Being, One and the Same, Everywhere as a Whole*** by Eyjólfur Emilsson and Steven Strange

Ennead **VI.8:** ***On the Voluntary and on the Free Will of the One*** by Kevin Corrigan and John D. Turner

ETHICS

Sentience and Sensibility: *A Conversation about Moral Philosophy* by Matthew R. Silliman

PHILOSOPHICAL FICTION

Pythagorean Crimes by Tefcros Michaelides

The Aristotle Quest: A Dana McCarter Trilogy. Book 1: Black Market Truth by Sharon M. Kaye

AUDIOBOOKS

The Iliad (unabridged) by Stanley Lombardo

The Odyssey (unabridged) by Stanley Lombardo

The Essential Homer by Stanley Lombardo

The Essential Iliad by Stanley Lombardo

FORTHCOMING

Ennead* I.2: *On Virtues by Suzanne Stern-Gillet

Ennead* I.3: *On Dialectic by Pauliina Remes

Ennead* I.4: *On Well-Being by Kieran McGroarty

Ennead* I.5: *On Whether Well Being Increases With Time by Danielle A. Layne

Ennead* I.8: *On the Nature and Source of Evil by Anne Sheppard

Ennead* II.4: *On Matter by Anthony A. Long

Ennead* II.7: *On Complete Blending by Robert Goulding

Ennead* II.8: *On Sight by Robert Goulding

Ennead* III.4: *On Our Allotted Guardian Spirit by Wiebke-Marie Stock

Ennead* III.5: *On Love by Sara Magrin

Ennead* III.6: *On Impassibility by Eleni Perdikouri

Ennead* III.7: *On Eternity and Time by László Bene

Ennead* III.8: *On Nature and Contemplation by George Karamanolis

Ennead* IV.6: *On Sense-Perception and Memory by Peter Lautner

Ennead* V.2, V.4, and V.6: *On the One and Intellect by Eleni Perdikouri

Ennead* V.3: *On the Knowing Hypostases by Marie-Élise Zovko

Ennead* V.8: *On Intelligible Beauty by Andrew Smith

Ennead* V.9: *On Intellect, Ideas, and Being by Matthias Vorwerk

Ennead* VI.1-2: *On the Genera of Being (I+II) by Damien Caluori and Regina Füchslin

Ennead* VI.3: *On the Genera of Being (III) by Riccardo Chiaradonna

Ennead* VI.7: *The Forms and the Good by Nicholas Banner

Ennead* VI.9: *On the Good or the One by Stephen R. L. Clark